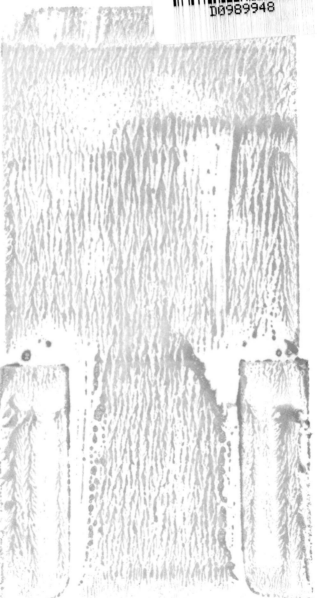

Around
Western Campfires

by JOSEPH "MACK" AXFORD

THE UNIVERSITY OF ARIZONA PRESS
Tucson   Arizona

About the Author

JOSEPH "MACK" AXFORD, onetime cowboy and cattleman in the neighborhood of Tombstone, Arizona, was always a man who knew his West. Coming from Michigan in 1894, Mack started work on cattle ranches at age fourteen, for ten dollars a month and room and board from an outfit at the head of the San Pedro River in Arizona Territory. His personal history paralleled the transition from pioneer to modern activities as Mack worked in mines along the Mexican border, guarded prisoners in the Cochise County Jail, filled in as surgeon at the County Hospital, and later became superintendent of the great herds of W. C. Greene's cattle company. Mack's adventures brought him into contact with Arizona characters—some of whom became famous as outlaws, and his advancing years revealed him as a born story teller of men and events in the Arizona borderlands of the young twentieth century. The year 1968 found Mack still in motion, not only as a teller of tales around the campfire, but as Parade Marshal for Tombstone's annual Helldorado celebration.

THE UNIVERSITY OF ARIZONA PRESS

Copyright © 1969
The Arizona Board of Regents
Library of Congress Catalog
Card No. 70-79583
Manufactured in the U.S.A.

To the late Frank B. Moson, Hereford, Arizona,
*   who taught me to ride and rope,*
and to my brother, Henry W. Axford, Rochester, Michigan,
*   who will always be sorry that he never knew*
the "Old West" as I lived and loved it

Contents

First Night in Bisbee and the First Job

When I arrived in Bisbee, Arizona, in April, 1894, I was fourteen years old, broke and trying to find something to do. I had tried the Copper Queen Mine, asking if they had anything that I could do, to which the foreman replied that the mine worked only adults, no kids.

In those days no one paid much attention to a kid inside a saloon, so the first evening found me huddled with a group of men around a potbellied stove in the White House saloon, as I remember the name. A gambler apparently about two-thirds drunk was bucking Faro at a table just to my left. The lookout was in his chair and it was elevated just enough to give him clear vision over the table. Suddenly the gambler whom they called Curley got up and cursing the dealer, jumped up on the case rack and kicked the dealer in the face. He then jumped off the table and went over to the bar. The lookout walked over to the bar and talked for a moment with a man wearing an apron who was evidently the owner. He nodded his head, the lookout returned to his chair and the Faro game continued. In a moment Curley returned to the table, threw down a gold piece and called for another stack of chips. The dealer nodded to the owner who came over and told Curley that until he sobered up he would not be allowed to play. As Curley turned away from the table, a gray-whiskered man alongside of me who had evidently smiled at Curley was attacked by him and knocked down with one blow, saying as he did so, "What are you grinning at, you old son of a b—?"

The old man, in falling, tipped over the stove, the stove pipe came down and the room filled with smoke. I remember helping him to his feet and how mad it made me at the moment to see the savage attack on this old man. The stove was righted and the stove pipe replaced when two shots were heard in the street. I rushed outside with the rest to a spot in the street a little further down from the saloon to where a cowpuncher I won't name had been shot off his horse by the gentleman who was town constable. Alongside the cowboy as he lay in the street was a canvas bag filled with silver. It seems the deceased had held up a Monte game somewhere up the street and had been shot by the officer in resisting arrest. After looking at the dead man I became sick and had to get off to one side for a moment. As my mind went over the night's excitement the thought came to me—"This is the West sure enough."

I had never seen the rough side of life and that night's doings were an eye opener. Several miners had talked to me about what I was doing there, a kid alone, and knew I was a homeless lad looking for a job. My first morning I was standing on the opposite side of the street from the Can Can Restaurant. A big six-foot rancher had just stepped out from the Can Can and stood for a moment picking his teeth. A miner called my attention to the rancher, told me he had a ranch out on the San Pedro River and suggested that I go over and tackle him for a job. I walked across the street and asked him if he had any work for a boy on his farm. He asked me where my home was and I told him at the moment it was wherever I hung my hat. He asked me where my parents were and I replied that they were both dead. He looked me straight in the eye and asked if I was hungry. I told him I had no money but needed a job badly. He grabbed my arm and led me into the restaurant where he told the waiter to give the kid a T-bone steak, French-fried potatoes and a hunk of pie, and he would be back in a moment to pay for it. He seated me at one of the tables and told me, "Kid, there is a big cowman named Packard in town and I am going to see if Pack will give you a job."

The rancher, who I learned from the waiter was named Watts, returned before I had finished the meal and told me to be at the O.K. Stable at three o'clock, that Packard would give me a job at ten dollars a month and found. It was about noon at the time; I immediately went to the O.K. Stable and waited until three for Watts and Packard to show up. Just at three o'clock Packard and Watts came driving up in a buckboard; it seemed that Watts had ridden in on horseback, Packard in his buckboard, and had figured out that the kid would be thrilled to ride Watts' horse, so Watts would ride with Packard in the rig. Watts told the stableman to saddle his horse and explained that I was to ride it to the ranch. The horse was, I learned later, a cinch-bound, spoiled animal, and often when cinched up too tight would rear and fall over backward when you attempted to mount. The stableman handed me the reins and just as I started to get on, the horse reared up and fell over backward with a crash on the barn floor. I managed to land on my feet but I could feel my hair trying to crawl out through the crown of my hat. Just then I heard Packard say, "Kid, the main thing is to keep your hind end right in the middle of the saddle." The stableman said he thought he knew what was the matter—that the horse was cinch-bound. He loosened the cinch, stepped up on the horse, spun him around a couple of times and getting off said he was all right now and would give me no trouble. The stableman helped me to mount and I was soon on my way for my first horseback ride, a distance of eighteen miles.

Packard told me to take the first righthand road down the canyon and they were away in a cloud of dust. I soon found that riding a horse was some job—Watts was a six-footer and I could not reach the stirrups. After several miles this way I finally figured that if I put my feet in the stirrup leather just at the top of the stirrup it would help a lot. I worked at it until I had both feet in place and this gave me a setup almost as good as real stirrups. It was a good thing that I had figured out the stirrup deal for I would have been thrown from the horse about an hour later if my feet had not been bound in by the stirrup leathers. It was now about four-thirty in the afternoon; as I was getting rather warm I took off my little coat and not knowing what else to do with it, hung it loose over the saddle horn. At a point where the San Pedro road goes around a limestone hill, a jack rabbit suddenly jumped out of the sage brush, the horse dipped low in shying to one side, dropping out from under my coat, leaving it in the middle of the road. Had my feet not been tightly secured in the stirrup leathers I would have been thrown. I was afraid to get off the horse in order to pick up my coat fearing I could not get on again, so I rode on and left the coat in the middle of the road.

I had no idea of a country road—I presumed it would end right at the ranch. By this time it was getting rather late; I had reached the bottom lands of the San Pedro and knew that the road was fenced on the river side but I had passed right on by the gate in the fence, which was the entrance to the ranch. Hearing someone holler I looked over and could see Watts and Packard standing in front of an old barn and I could make out the word "gate." Turning in the saddle I looked back and could see a break in the fence where two high posts were fastened across the top with a long pole and realized this was the gate. I rode back to the gate and had considerable trouble getting my feet out of the stirrup straps as my legs were so stiff and sore; finally making it, I slid off the horse and immediately collapsed, as my knees gave way and for a moment would not support my body. I crawled to the gate and taking hold of the wire pulled myself erect and fought until I got the gate open. Watts reached me just as the gate fell open and helped me down to the house.

This was the start of my life in the saddle and my first ride of eitheen miles will always be remembered as the hardest ride of all. I have since covered fifty miles in a day and forty was often just a day's work in a saddle but the first eighteen miles tops them all.

The next morning I was put to irrigating an alfalfa field with a Mexican to show me what to do. In about a week, Packard's wagon boss, Henry Ashton, pulled in from Mexico with about 700 head of mixed cattle which Packard had purchased in Old Mexico. I might say at this point that Packard's ranch "The Half Moon" was located on the headwaters of the San Pedro River about seven or eight miles north of the international boundary line separating the two countries. Packard turned me over to his wagon boss telling him, "Ashton, here is a kid that I think you can use; he should make a good horse wrangler." We were immediately put to work building a corral about two miles west of the ranch on what was called the Huachuca Flat. When the corral was finished a cowboy by the name of Grant Lewis took charge of a Mexican rider and me; we put up a tent fairly close to the corral which we had built, the tent to hold our bedding, grub supplies and cooking utensils. We were to day-herd the 700 head of cattle on the flat land which was covered with heavy Grama grass, driving them each day to the San Pedro River for water. In the meantime Henry Ashton had taken his outfit back to Old Mexico after more cattle which had been purchased.

The first month passed quickly; Packard rode out and paid me my first money, a ten-dollar gold piece. I expected something else, as I understood that I was to be paid ten dollars and found. I did not know what "found" was but I knew it had not been paid, whatever it was. However I kept my own counsel and waited to find out what it was that Mr. Packard had overlooked paying me.

My duties consisted, in addition to the regular herding duties, of always being the one to rustle wood for the camp fire on which we cooked, and when sent in each day to build the fire I was to put on the coffee pot with the right amount of water, and the two Dutch ovens. Grant Lewis did the cooking, and the Mexican washed up the dishes. In this way we all had a share of the work to be done. Another month went by and Mr. Packard again came out to pay me another ten dollars. I now had two ten dollar gold pieces, but I still was not given the found. At this point I thought Mr. Packard was deliberately withholding something that was due me. Again I kept my mouth shut and waited.

Soon Ashton returned with an additional 500 head of mixed cattle, and we were told that we were to trail the cattle overland to Phoenix, Arizona, where Packard had another ranch. It took a day or two to get organized; we then started north down the San Pedro River on our way to Phoenix. The horse herd was turned over to me as my responsibility and Henry Ashton said he would look after me until I understood just what my duties were to be. I was usually told to go ahead of the cattle but to keep in sight at all times, should it be necessary for one of the boys to have to change horses. I bet I counted those horses twenty-five or thirty times each day, for that was the only way I could tell whether I had lost any. We made it just above Fairbank that first day. As we were short of hands, it was necessary to stand guard half the night around the cattle and I had to help out with this, for we always hobbled the horses at night. The second night was spent opposite Saint David, a Mormon settlement; the third day we were met a few miles out of Benson by Mr. Packard and told to put the cattle in the shipping pens in Benson, as he had sold the cattle to a California buyer and we were to load them out that night. I had commenced to like the work on the trail and was a little disappointed when we had to turn back at Benson.

As soon as we returned to the ranch we immediately got ready to start rounding up cattle in Old Mexico, working first on the southern side of the San José Mountains. We were joined by several other cattlemen, among them Ben Sneed who represented the OH outfit which branded OH on the left hip and this outfit was owned by Ed Roberts who originally came from Oregon, to the southwest. The following story will give you some idea of Old Ed Roberts who was a hard man to beat in a horse trade. Old Ed was a cattle buyer working out of Roseburg, Oregon, in the early days and was considered the keenest judge of cattle and horses in the Oregon country. Ed was also an inveterate whittler, always keeping his knife in top condition, and would start whittling when engaged in a battle of wits over prices or at his favorite pastime, horse trading. A large number of his purchases were made on the eastern side of the mountains in the Lakeview and Klamath country. At the time of this story, Ed had bargained to purchase a number of steers near Lakeview and was to take delivery on a certain day, so had driven over a day or two ahead of time. Arriving at the ranch he found that it would be several days before the cattle would all be rounded up so Ed spent some time at the ranch with the father of the boys who were selling the cattle. As the days were long Ed and the old man used to sit in the sun out by the barn discussing this and that and always Ed would pick up a piece of wood and start his continuous whittling. One day the old man bantered Ed for a horse trade, said he had a horse that would match up better with Ed's than the horse he had, and after the usual dickering, a trade was made, with Roberts getting forty dollars cash difference. That same day the old man's sons arrived with the steers; Ed had a ten percent cut after trimming out cripples and off-color cattle; the boys were then to drive them to the top of the mountain where Ed would receive and finish paying for them. Roberts hitched up his new horse and started for home.

A couple of days later the old man thought he would

try out his new horse, hitched him up and soon found out that Roberts had way the best of the trade. He had quite a sense of humor and remembered that Ed was always whittling when he was talking trade, so he sawed up a number of wood blocks, packed them in a tomato case, wrote one line on a piece of paper which he placed in the middle of the box and expressed it C.O.D. to Ed at Roseburg. In those days all express had to go south by way of Reno, Nevada, to Sacramento, then north to Roseburg.

A few days after this Ed drove into town after some groceries and was advised that the express office had a package for him. Ed drove down on his way home, paid the $6.80 charges, tossed the box in the back of the buckboard and drove home. His wife and daughter came out to help him in with the supplies. His daughter, Bird, brought in the express box and asked her father what was in it. Ed answered, "I don't know." Bird said, "Ain't you going to open it, papa?" Ed said, "You open it." Bird got a hammer and pounded off the lid, saw the wooden blocks and started tossing them out, when she found the sheet of paper on which was written the one line "Whittle, you son of a b—, whittle."

The Roberts family always loved this story.

I Rope My First Big Steer

We had been across the line into Mexico rounding up for a month or more. The international boundary line was unfenced and American and Mexican cattle alike strayed back and forth between the two countries. We finally finished our work and had about six hundred head of mixed cattle owned by different Americans to drive back to Arizona Territory. I was the horse wrangler for the Americans and little Pedro Gonzales, a Mexican boy about my age, was the Mexican wrangler. Our duties were to ride herd on the horses in the daytime, taking the horses to the places designated as the roundup ground, in order for the riders to change from the horses used on the roundup to the better trained horses to be used in cutting the cattle found outside the roundup itself into the bunch to be held and returned to their home ranges.

The remuda horses were always hobbled at night to keep them from straying off during the night and a special detail of riders got up early each morning to bring in the horses for the riders to catch their day horses out of. The horses were then turned over to Pedro and me to look after during the day. This stray herd, as it was called, also required night herding; a watch of two hours usually was necessary during the night; sometimes, however, if the crew was shorthanded the night was divided into two shifts of half the night each.

This Mexico work called for half the night to be spent riding herd on the strays; only once in a while were we lucky enough to find a corral to put the stray herd in. When a corral was available Pedro and I always managed to be on hand to help put the cattle inside the corral. Here often a couple of calves would break away and make a run for it, allowing Pedro and me to get a little roping practice on the young calves. This was great fun for us.

The day arrived when the roundup work was over and we started back with the six hundred head of mixed cattle. After crossing the line into Arizona, the first night was to be spent at the Fike Ranch on Green Bush Draw, about three miles from where the town of Naco now stands. The cinch was loose on the little buckskin horse which I was riding and as I would be roping only a small calf, should one break back, I neglected to tighten the cinch. At the Fike Ranch was a large circular corral and permission had been obtained from Mrs. Fike to use the corral for the cattle.

When we separated in Mexico I had bade good-bye to Pedro, so he was not available to help should it be needed. So I rode into help corral the cattle. To make a long story short, no calves broke back from the corral but two steers did, one a medium-size two year old and the other a big steer with wide horns and weighing about eleven or twelve hundred pounds. Up to this moment I had never roped a big animal. A puncher named Jim Toutin turned back with me after the two steers; before I could call to him to rope the bigger steer, he had already piled his rope on the two year old, leaving the big steer for me.

I sailed after this steer with all the canvas on, and by the time I reached it had what old-time Texans call a Blocker loop, my rope tied fast to the horn, which was the custom where double cinch saddles were used. I made a beautiful throw, the big loop going over the steer's head perfectly, but before I could pull up the slack, he stepped his front feet through the loop and I had him around the middle. When the steer hit the end of the rope I rode the saddle up over the horse's head taking the bridle off the horse as the saddle went over. The saddle caught on a mesquite root breaking the rope. I picked up the saddle and carried it to the chuck wagon which was only about one hundred and fifty feet away. When I laid the saddle down I was surprised to find that the cinch had not broken, in fact was still connected to the latigo. What had happened was the cinch was loose enough that it had skimmed over the horse's head and both front legs without breaking. I lived several years before I saw this accident duplicated. Joe Rhodes, roping a yearling on the steep slope of a hill, had his saddle skim over his horse's head without undoing or breaking the cinch.

I believe that I forgot to mention that Ben Sneed, who was a stepson of old Ed Roberts, was wagon boss on this, my first roundup, and the boys kept kidding him about his horse race with Uncle Billy Plaster which had taken place the year before. Here is the story as I heard it. Star Bay was one of the top cow horses of the OH outfit whose range covered the area in Cochise County, Arizona Territory along the Mexican border lying west of the town of Naco, and on the headwaters of the San Pedro River.

The OH spread was owned by Ed Roberts, whom you have already met as the inveterate whittler in the horse-trading story. Ed owned around 5,000 head of mixed cattle, and worked about three cowboys through the spring, summer, and fall, cutting down to one man to look after things through the winter months. The winter job was always reserved for Ben Sneed who was Mrs. Roberts' son by a former marriage. Sneed usually kept one of the top horses to ride throughout the winter; this horse was kept up and fed grain in order to keep him in top condition. Star Bay was originally a Riggs horse bought from the Riggs ranch which operated on the east side of Sulphur Springs Valley about twenty miles south of the town of Willcox, Arizona. The Riggs had two horse brands, one a star on left thigh, low down, and a capital R. The capital R was owned by Miss Rhoda Riggs, a daughter. Both brands of horses were in great demand by other cow outfits, for the horses were natural cow horses and easily broken to ride.

Star Bay was the top horse in Sneed's mount and in addition was the fastest cow horse on the San Pedro and had easily beaten all comers in the races which were always held in the first week of the spring and fall roundups. The usual work of the winter hand was to ride the range, keeping track of the cattle and to brand all calves found unbranded. It was necessary to rope these unbranded calves on the open range, which called for a top horse to do the job. So Sneed kept Star Bay for his winter horse. Sneed, unknown to his stepfather, was quite a card player and a well-trained judge of hard liquor.

The OH headquarters were located about four and a half miles north of the Mexican border and in the years of this story were unfenced, cattle ranging on both sides of the international boundary line. About four miles inside Mexico was the little Mexican town of San Pedro (which later became part of the famous Greene cattle holdings), and in the town a Frenchman known as Mormalahue had a little store and canteen where groceries and liquor were sold. On the American side, almost astride of the line between the two countries, Uncle Billy Plaster had his little ranch consisting of a small adobe house and corral and horse pasture. Uncle Billy ran a few head of cattle.

Sneed in riding up to San Pedro had to pass within a few yards of Plaster's house. After breakfast he would saddle Star Bay and tie on a gunny sack nosebag which contained a feed of rolled barley for Star Bay's midday meal. After giving the range close up a rapid glance Sneed would head for San Pedro and Mormalahue's. In front of the store was a hitching rack at which Star Bay spent hour after hour and always was fed his feed of rolled barley. Old Uncle Billy Plaster noticed Sneed riding by, day after day, followed Sneed into San Pedro several times and always found Star Bay tied up in front of the canteen and usually with his nosebag still on.

The spring roundup was started at the Elías Ranch a few miles south of San Pedro and was to work north into the American territory. Usually the first day of the roundup called for several races between the riders. When the usual bickering started over who had the fastest horse most cowboys had little to offer against Star Bay but Uncle Billy once in a while was overheard to remark,

"I've got a horse which I think can beat Star Bay." These remarks in time reached the ears of Ben Sneed. As Sneed was a natural gambler, a cinch horse race had a lot of appeal, so he sought out Uncle Billy and bantered him for a race. Uncle Billy's answer always was, "I think I have a horse that can beat Star Bay, but give me time to think it over." Uncle Billy knew it would be several days before the roundup would reach the town of San Pedro and he was waiting for the day. He needled Sneed from time to time and had him worked up to such a pitch that he wanted to bet three hundred Star Bay could beat any horse in the remuda.

Some of the boys told Sneed that Uncle Billy said there was not a quarter-mile stretch of level land to run on and he would not run until such a spot was found. The morning after the roundup arrived in San Pedro, Sneed again got after Uncle Billy and called attention to the Main Street which was long enough and level enough. Uncle Billy and Sneed walked out on the street to look things over. "Which way would you run, Sneed?" asked Uncle Billy. "Why, hell," said Sneed, "run straight through the town, have the finish line about a hundred feet south of Mormalahue's." Sneed wanted the race to finish close to the tavern so he could celebrate his victory in the proper manner.

The distance was measured off and the finish line marked as Sneed suggested. Little did Sneed suspect that if he had insisted on running the other way, Uncle Billy would not have bet. Uncle Billy covered Sneed's three hundred and the race was on. Both horses broke at the start but when half of the distance had been covered Star Bay was about three lengths in the lead and it was easily seen that Uncle Billy's horse was no match for Star Bay. At this point several cowboys were heard to remark,

"Why on earth did Uncle Billy make this bet!" Star Bay was a good five lengths ahead, when opposite the hitching rack in front Mormalahue's he suddenly bolted, ran up to the hitching post and stopped. Uncle Billy's horse ran on through, an easy victor.

Sneed was never able to live down the ribbing he took over this race, and Ed Roberts never kept him for his winter man after that. Uncle Billy often said after the race that it was the first time in his life he was able to bet on what he thought was a sure thing—he knew that horses, like people, are creatures of habit. He knew Star Bay would stop at the hitching rack where he had been fed his grain so many times.

After the roundup we returned to the Packard Ranch and I went back to irrigating. It was about this time that I learned that "found" meant my bed and board and that Packard had not been withholding anything from me.

We often had hunters for quail, rabbits and ducks come to the ranch and they were most always given permission to hunt. Sometimes they would say overnight and usually had their campfires in one corner of the corral, where they were often joined by the ranch hands to listen to the gossip and stories so often told at such gatherings. It was here that I heard the story of when the employe proved smarter. It concerned a mine foreman whose name, if my memory is correct, was Wes Howell, Superintendent of the Copper Queen Mine in Bisbee, Arizona. The ore was being worked in an open pit—this "glory hole" is still there with the old tunnel which Wes Howell drove back into the mountain, the entrance closed and locked up. It seems that from the looks of things the ore body was pinching out; at least the mining engineer in charge, who lived somewhere in the East, after making a careful inspection of the ore body on one of his periodical trips, had given orders to work out the ore in the glory hole and when this was done to close down the mine. Wes Howell however had different ideas. As soon as the engineer left, he started a tunnel following a small mineralized seam back into the mountain and kept the work going. Whenever the company engineer was scheduled to arrive he had the tunnel mouth boarded up and the face completely covered with rock waste which hid the work from the prying eyes of the engineer. The miners all joined in with the game, for a game it was, which would mean a lot to the men if Howell was lucky enough to open up another body of ore with the stolen tunnel. You have no doubt guessed it by now. Before the glory hole was worked out Howell ran into what was known as the famous Southwest stope, an immense body of ore which kept the Copper Queen working for many years and probably contributed most to making the Phelps Dodge Company in due time one of the world's great copper producers. If you ever go to Bisbee, walk up to the old glory hole; you will see the old tunnel entrance I have told you about.

As of 1964, this canyon where the glory hole was located had produced $1,300,000,000 worth of ore.

I Meet the W.C. Greene Family

About this time the boys were all excited about a dance which was to be held at Uncle Billy Plaster's place which was up the river a few miles. Among the boys at the ranch was an Irish kid, Jim Moran, and as Jim was also an orphan we had something in common and soon became good friends. Saturday night came, the night of the dance, and I was surrounded by the boys led by Jim Moran, all insisting that I go to the dance with them. "I can't go, boys, I have no coat to wear," having lost my coat between Bisbee and the ranch when I first went to work for Packard. "We'll soon fix that" said Moran, grabbing a coat off a nail on the wall and hustling me into it. "Fits you perfect, Mack," said Jim turning me around several times so the boys could enjoy the fit. So I saddled up and we were on our way to my first dance.

As I did not know how to dance I spent my time in the kitchen. Jim would rush out once in a while and grabbing me by the arm would pull me into the front room and introduce me to someone. I noticed that Jim always turned me around a couple of times as if showing off the fit of the coat. The night was about half gone when Jim and a bunch of the boys came in and very seriously asked me what in hell I had on the back of my coat. I answered "I don't know, but will soon find out." Taking the coat off, I found that at some not too distant date the coat had been hung up in a chicken house. I then understood why Moran always turned me around a couple of times whenever he got me in the front room. I will always believe that it was because all the boys liked me that I was not saddled with a nickname then and there.

A few days after the dance we were all still sitting around the table in the kitchen when a young man about my age knocked on the door and was introduced to us by Mr. Packard as young Frank Moson, whose mother owned the adjoining ranch of OR cattle. Moson told Packard that his mother had sent him down to collect for several OR steers which Packard had shipped out. Packard told him that he would not pay for the steers at that time and young Moson told him just what he and his mother thought about it. After Moson left, Packard said that Bill Greene who was married to Frank's mother had borrowed some money from him and he was going to hold the money for Mrs. Greene's cattle for the payment.

A few days after this I again met young Moson and he

talked me into making my home with them. The Greene family at that time consisted of Mrs. W. C. Greene, who owned the ranch and OR brand of cattle; a son and daughter by a previous marriage, Frank and Virginia Moson; and two daughters by Mr. Greene, Ella and Eva.

Mrs. Greene had dammed the San Pedro River and was irrigating at that time over a hundred acres of bottom land. William Cornell Greene, the husband, spent most of his time in Mexico, mining and trying to make up the loss of a large sum of money for a shipment of Mrs. Greene's cattle which Greene claimed were never paid for. Mrs. Greene told him to get out and hustle and try to pay back to the children what he had lost.

I lived with the Greene family over a year and was offered a job with the Erie Cattle Company operating in Sulphur Springs Valley. This was a job as a cowhand paying thirty dollars a month and board. Shortly after I left the Greene family, I heard the dam on the river was blown up. Now Greene had been down in Mexico for several months looking for a way to reimburse the estate. Mrs. Greene had dammed up the San Pedro Creek about three-quarters of a mile above the ranch and had several fields of alfalfa growing from the water brought in by a ditch from the dam. Jim Burnett had an adjoining ranch about one-and-a-half miles down the river from the Greene Ranch. The Greene dam had been in place for several years and was protected by a water right.

As long as Burnett was just using his holdings for pasture everything was all right, but one day he brought in a couple of Chinese gardeners who made a dam in the river and commenced to use water from the San Pedro. In the summertime the children used to swim in the river about one-half mile below the Greene dam—they had always used the same place which was never over waist-deep and had a sandy beach. Burnett's Chinamen, evidently bent on getting more water from the river, were blamed for destroying Mrs. Greene's dam; anyway the dam went out and the water washed a deep hole where the children had been in the habit of swimming.

One day a friend's daughter was visiting the Greene family, and the three girls, Eva, Ella and Katie Corcoran, went down to the river to take a swim. When the Corcoran girl stepped into the river, instead of finding shallow water, she stepped into a deep hole which had been washed out when the dam went out. Ella Greene jumped in to help the Corcoran girl and both girls were drowned, Eva running back to the house to give the alarm. A rider was dispatched to Mexico to find Greene and advise him of the tragedy. In a few days Mr. Greene came driving in, stopping just long enough at the ranch to change teams and was told that Jim Burnett's men had caused the tragedy by destroying the dam.

Greene immediately left for Tombstone. Driving up to the OK Stables he found Burnett seated in a chair talking to John Montgomery. Green got out of the buggy and as he approached Burnett, Burnett threw his hands back in order to get up from the chair and Greene shot him just as he raised up, killing him instantly. Greene, raising his hand over Burnett's body said, "God's will be done," and turning, walked down to the court house and surrendered to Scott White, the sheriff. By the next morning a half-million dollars was available to pay Greene's bail. He was tried and found not guilty—stating that when Burnett threw his hands back in order to raise himself from the chair he thought Burnett was going after his gun.

I worked for W. C. Greene for several years after this episode and therefore I have my own opinions as to what were the facts in this case. Since Greene's family did lay the blame for the drowning on Burnett, it is not surprising that many people cling to the idea that Greene was quite determined to seek revenge for the death of his beloved daughter.

I stayed with the Erie Cattle Company under Wagon Boss Bob Johnson until the fall work was finished and then teamed up with Tom Capehart and Henry Marshall to work that winter breaking a bunch of broncs. Any cowboy who has had the experience of breaking a bunch of horses to saddle should enjoy this story. A young kid, especially if he is green and new to the work, has always been on the receiving end of the many jokes which cowhands like to play on the hero-worshipping kid. Tom Capehart was such a hero at the time, for Tom was a noted bronco stomper; he had ridden the celebrated outlaw Glencoe of the San Simon outifit, even after he had unhorsed all of their top hands. Glencoe was still mentioned years later as one of Arizona's worst buckers.

Henry Marshall, the second member of our trio, was a fair to middling cowhand, more noted for his pleasant disposition and for being a steady and hard worker. I, the butt of all cowboy jokes, was the third member, sixteen years of age, strong and eager to learn. All three of us had been working for the Erie Cattle Company, an outfit owned by a group of Pennsylvania Dutch and under the supervision of Bob Johnson, our boss. The fall work was over and Johnson had picked his men for the winter work, which consisted of range branding the few calves which the roundup had missed, repairing fences, rustling wood for the different branding pens, and the breaking of any unbroken horses which the outfit had on hand.

The company had recently purchased two carloads of broncs from some outfit in Colorado and had them running loose in a large horse pasture located in the foothills of the San Simon Valley. Johnson made a deal with Capehart and Marshall to break out this bunch of horses at five dollars per head. As a kid is handy to have around for camp chores, such as rustling wood for the cookstove, and the like, Capehart asked me to join them and offered to cut me in on the deal. As this gave me an opportunity to learn under one of the great cowhands, I readily accepted. Our first evening was spent in checking over our gear and in discussing the different duties. Capehart and Marshall were to do the cooking, I was to take care of the dishwashing, keep the cabin clean and rustle the wood.

While discussing how we would ride the horses Capehart suggested that as I was the youngest and had never ridden broncs before, he would ride first saddle, Marshall the second saddle and I was to ride the third saddle. This sounded good to me; the boys were kind enough to take what appeared to me the worst end of the bargain, in order to give the kid the best of it. There were forty-six head of horses to be broken gentle to saddle and bridle. We all pitched in of course to help with the horses when they were first roped. The corral was circular, made of heavy juniper posts about eight feet in height with a snubbing post in the center. One of us would catch the horse we wanted by the forefeet as they came charging by; when a catch was made the one closest to the roper would pile on to help the roper, the horse would be thrown, then Capehart would take over, slip a hackamore over the nose and head, and if the horse was not too snaky we would let him up, take a wrap or two around the snubbing post and the first lesson given.

This first work was usually done by Capehart who, talking in kind tones to the horse, would approach him on the left side and if the horse was not too wild, slip a rope over his neck just ahead of the shoulders tied in a liberal loop with a bowline, then slipping a loop through this neck rope, snare the left hind foot, drawing this loop until the left foot was about six inches from the ground. This left the horse on three legs and helpless as far as being able to do much damage. In this position he could not kick or paw with his front feet.

Usually Marshall would take over at this time and still talking kindly to the horse slap a saddle blanket on his back, take it off, slap it on him time and again until the horse realized that the blanket was not going to hurt him; it was also customary to let the horse smell of the blanket and look it over. If the horse was snaky the blanket treatment was continued until it was pretty well subdued and tired out.

At this point Capehart would take over, approaching with the cinch and right stirrup up over the seat of the saddle, set the saddle up on the horse's back letting the cinch and the right stirrup down easily, reach under the horse's belly, catch hold of the cinch and proceed to tighten it. The horse would try to buck when he felt the cinch tighten but with one foot tied up he was helpless. Capehart would then usually get up and down from the saddle several times until the horse accepted this without much struggle. Capehart never used a blind on a horse—the horse was at all times able to see what was being done.

The loop was taken off the hind leg, the rope released

from the snubbing post and the horse allowed to buck it out. By this time he was a very tired horse. Then Capehart riding first saddle would get on the horse and ride him around in the corral for a while. Next the horse would be taken out and staked to a log which he could drag a little and left staked this way over night. This soon teaches a horse to respect a rope; he will try to run off but will usually be thrown when he reaches the end of the rope. A time or two of this will cause the horse to stop the moment he feels a rope around his neck, as a horse learns quickly.

The next day would be Marshall's turn to ride second saddle and Capehart would take on a new horse for the first saddle. The third day would be my time to ride. You would think that after two saddles I would have the easiest time, but for some reason the horses would most always buck with me, once in a while with Marshall on second saddle but seldom with Capehart on first saddle. Capehart said he could not understand why this was so, said that maybe I did not talk enough to the horse and called my attention to the fact that he always kept up a chatter when around a horse. Well I did some pretty tall talking but it did not seem to help—the darn critters always bucked with me.

One day one of the ranch hands, named Perkins, came to the pasture to get a change of horses; the next morning Capehart told me to help Perkins ride the pasture for the horse he wanted. Perkins asked, "How you getting along, kid, with your first time breaking horses?" "Well," I said, "if riding pitching horses is going to help I will soon be as good a rider as Capehart." "How's that?" "Well, where the horses never pitch with Capehart, seldom with Marshall, they always pitch when I ride them." "How you riding them?" asked Perkins. I told him that

Capehart rode first saddle, Marshall second and I rode the third saddle. Perkins doubled up on his horse with laughter. "Kid," he said, "they're working you." He then explained that the horse is usually worn down too tired to buck on first saddle, the second saddle they are apt to buck, but the third saddle, changing riders, with a new rider a horse will most always buck. "You change this, kid, pick your own horse, ride him straight through— don't let them work you any more."

After Perkins left I held a conference with Capehart and Marshall, told them that from now on I was riding first, second and third saddle—no more of this third saddle business for me. Capehart doubled up with laughter. "Kid," he said, "it did not take you too long to wake up." Anyway when I finished my education that winter under the able teaching of Capehart and Marshall I felt that the tuition I paid was well worth it.

The Night I Grew Up

We all went back to work for Johnson in the spring. After spring branding was through I teamed up with Clay McGonegal to range-brand any calves missed by the spring roundup. Clay and I were camped at Moody Springs in upper San Simon Valley—a spring in the open valley just three-fourths of a mile outside the mouth of Price Canyon. This canyon, at its mouth, is a beautiful spot, the waterway running through open grasslands with scattered oak trees, and winding up between narrow rock walls as it enters the main range of the Chiricahua Mountains to the north.

Moody Springs was a favorite camping spot for range riders and roundup crews and much used by the United States Cavalry when in the vicinity on the trail of Apache

Indian renegades from the San Carlos Reservation. Across the valley east from this spot is Skeleton Canyon where Geronimo was captured several years before. The famous Apache Kid was on the rampage and often used the Apache Trail taken by the Indians when traveling south into Mexico. This trail was along the east slope of the Chiricahua Mountains.

A few days before this wild night of mine, McGonegal and I were trailing the tracks of a herd of cows and calves which evidently were watering somewhere further up Price Canyon. It was about four o'clock in the afternoon. Already the shadow of the Chiricahuas was halfway across the valley, the canyon had suddenly narrowed to what appeared to be almost a box. However, as the tracks of the cattle continued on, we felt that the canyon must turn to the right at a point we could see several yards ahead.

The floor of the canyon was solid rock at this point. As our horses were shod, we made quite a clatter as we rode onto the rock bottom. At this moment we heard an Indian speak just around the bend of the canyon which we could then see turned abruptly to the right. He was immediately answered by another Indian further up the canyon. Clay and I checked our horses and both spoke the one word "Indians." We then wheeled and started our run out of the canyon. Oldtimers had often told us that one never surprises an Apache, and as we turned to run we felt sure that we would be fired upon. However nothing happened. We made it out to the mouth of the canyon in record time. That night we moved our camp into the Erie Cattle Company pasture where we spent the night.

A few days later, finding our grub supply was getting low, McGonegal agreed to make a trip into headquarters ranch for a supply of food while I was to ride down to the San Simon Cattle Company horse pasture where some San Simon cowhands I knew were camped, and spend the night with them instead of making the long trip after supplies with McGonegal. Some weeks before, a prospector named Hand had been killed in Cave Creek, where the Indian had waited on top of Hand's dugout cabin for him to come out in the morning. This killing of Hand was credited to the Apache Kid who was running loose at that time. Cave Creek was a canyon running from the Chiricahua Mountains eastward into the San Simon Valley and about ten miles north of the San Simon horse pasture where I intended to stay that night with the boys.

I arrived at the horse camp about five in the evening. The boys were evidently still out somewhere but I felt sure they would soon come in. The cabin was supplied with plenty of grub and three beds well covered with bedding. After checking the cabin I went out to the woodpile and cut a couple armfuls of wood. By this time it was getting rather late and I commenced to wonder what had happened to the boys. Sensing that they might have gone to the main ranch and not liking to keep my horse up for the night in the corral without feed, I saddled him up and ran in a bunch of saddle horses which I could see grazing in the pasture. I caught a flea-bitten gray San Simon horse for the night horse and hobbled my horse so he could still feed and not wander far away.

The horse pasture was located along the east side of the Chiricahuas and extended about one mile out into the valley. In this way it was necessary to fence only three sides of the pasture, the mountains making a natural fence on the west. In the southeast corner of the pasture were located the windmill, corral, and a one-room cabin made out of old railroad ties stood on end. The roof was made out of the same material with the ties extended each way from a ridge pole in the center and the ties on top covered with about two feet of dirt. This gave a cabin about ten by twelve feet in size.

The inside of the cabin had a place for three narrow bunks. The cookstove was a No. 7 wood stove sitting on a box filled with dirt, which took the place of legs. The stove pipe went straight up through the dirt roof. The room had one small window and one board door. The door was fastened on the inside by a two-by-four which was dropped into two pieces of iron with offsets, fastened one on each side of the door.

I had cut sign around the cabin and had come to the conclusion that the boys had been gone for a couple or three days as there were no fresh tracks and no leftovers from cooking, such as boiled potatoes or beans. It was too late to go any place as the nearest ranch was twenty miles down the valley, so I was stuck for the night. I built up a fire in the stove, got a bucket of fresh water from the windmill and proceeded to get supper. I made up a batch of frying-pan bread, fried some spuds in bacon grease and set the coffee pot on. After what I called a grand meal, I washed up the dishes, replenished the wood box, lit the kerosene lamp and was looking through some old magazines when the gray horse which I had shut up loose in the corral commenced to cut up. He would charge across the corral letting out a snort as if he was scared of something. Oldtimers had told me that if your night horse cuts up as if scared, it is one of two things, he either smells a mountain lion or bear, or it's Indians.

I slipped another cartridge into my Colt 45, making it

a six-full, blew out the lamp and slipped outside alongside the corral, figuring that if it was Indians they were probably after the horse. The horse finally quieted down and, as the evening was very chilly, I got rather cold and went back to the cabin. Thinking that probably a lion or a bear had crossed through, I dismissed the Indian side of it, lit the lamp and started again on the magazines. Suddenly I heard a scraping that sounded like somebody was climbing up on the roof of the cabin. I had dropped the two-by-four into position when I came in, so the door was securely fastened. It then flashed into my mind about the Indian who was on top of Hand's dugout waiting for him to come out in the morning. I had blown out the lamp the moment I heard the Indian climbing up on the roof, leaving the room in complete darkness. For a moment I was a badly scared boy. I had pulled the 45 from its scabbard and blown out the lamp almost in the same motion, and for several moments stood quietly in the middle of the cabin with the six-shooter in my hand, not knowing what to do. In a few minutes I got hold of myself and my mind commenced to figure things out. I knew I was in a bad position, alone, with an Indian on the roof. I remembered that I had often heard oldtimers mention that the Apache never attacked at night. He would set himself as he had with the prospector Hand and patiently wait for you to come out in the morning. This thought quieted me somewhat so I started to get ready to spend the night, firmly believing I would be safe until morning. I took the bedding from one of the bunks and made the bed on the floor behind the dirt box on which the stove rested. This put the stove box between me and the door and would give me some protection should the attack be made through the door.

For several hours I lay awake, still a badly scared kid. Sleep finally came and when daylight awakened me, my immediate thoughts were that the Indian was up there waiting for me to come out. I made no attempt to cook breakfast but instead nibbled on part of the frying-pan bread left over from supper. As it was the month of September the nights were rather cold. I wrapped one of the blankets around me, still staying on the bed behind the stove. An hour or two passed. By looking through a crack between the ties, I could make out the horse in the corral. As the horse seemed to be contented I figured that what little breeze was blowing was not in the direction of the horse. I commenced to get a little impatient, and realized that something had to happen. I finally worked out a plan of action. I figured that the Indian on top of the roof all night would no doubt be stiff and cold and that I had the advantage. I could open the door quietly and with six-shooter in hand make a running jump out the door, quickly cover the roof with the gun and, if lucky, get that Indian before he could get into action. I eased the two-by-four from the door, took a running jump out of the cabin and covered the roof with a cocked six-shooter. To my surprise, a large tiger tomcat raised up and greeted me with a friendly "Meow." My reaction here was rather funny. I was certainly more than glad to see a cat instead of an Indian, but I was also rather mad about it.

I found later that the San Simon boys had been gone for several days. The cat had no doubt been out rustling something to eat and was not in evidence when I arrived. I also learned that the boys had made a bed for the cat of gunny sacks placed near where the stove pipe went up through the roof and had leaned a tie against the building to aid it in getting up on the roof. It was the cat clawing his way up that gave the sound of clothes scraping which made things sound so real. Needless to say, I cooked up another batch of frying-pan bread for the cat, leaving him several days' supply to tide him over, should the boys be delayed longer. When I left, the cat followed me to the gate and I gave him another hug before mounting my horse and riding back to join McGonegal.

I had often wondered just what I would do if called upon to meet someone in a battle where six-shooters were to be used. I had listened to stories of different fights where someone had been killed, and greatly admired one who had the nerve to go. This night, with its long hours, when I was a badly scared kid, yet figured out a way to meet the situation and having the nerve to start the fight—this night separated me from the boys.

The Four-Bar Outfit

Shortly after this the Erie Cattle Company sold all its cattle, having eighteen months in which to make delivery, the cattle to be trailed to the railroad at Willcox and shipped. While gathering the cattle to be shipped we worked through the 4-Bar Range, then in charge of Uncle Jimmy Cox, who was a noted wit. Our outfit was camped at the 4-Bar headquarters when the following episode took place.

The 4-Bar outfit located in the middle of Sulphur Springs Valley in Cochise County, Arizona, was owned by a group living somewhere on the eastern shores of the United States and was rodded by an old time cowman, James Cox, called by one and all Uncle Jimmy Cox. The fall roundup was just starting and a couple of the eastern

owners had made the trip out to Arizona in order to see
for the first time a western cow outfit in operation and
also the holdings from which had been coming the rich
profits for many years. Uncle Jimmy was in his element
and enjoying to a great degree his role as foreman of the
outfit, busily explaining to the tenderfoot owners the ins
and outs of the cattle business. Most of us had been
introduced to the two men, usually with some comment
by Uncle Jimmy such as "this is our horse wrangler—our
roundup cook, etc." A couple of the boys were out on
the range after a bunch of saddle horses which were still
out and which were badly needed for the fall work about
to get started. Just before noon Bradshaw and Piatt, the
two men after the horses, came in with the missing
animals. This of course called for an introduction by
Uncle Jimmy. I happened to be about twenty feet away
when Piatt and Bradshaw rode up. I heard Uncle Jimmy
say, "You see the fellow on the red roan? That's John
Piatt, my top hand." Piatt and Bradshaw were introduced
and Uncle Jimmy turned to Piatt, asking him why he had
not fixed the fence around the tank at the Double
Windmills, saying, "I told you a week or so ago to fix
that fence, John, and it's still not fixed." "Well, Uncle
Jimmy," said Piatt, "I rode around the fence several
times and could not find a way to do it on horseback."
As Piatt and Bradshaw rode away I heard Uncle Jimmy
again remark, "That's my top hand." Unless it was a real
emergency, a top hand in those days usually shied away
from posthole digging, usually was an expert roper, and
would not do anything which could not be done on
horseback. But should an emergency arise, you will find
the top hand well in the lead doing his duty as called for,
no matter what the danger.

The 4-Bar headquarters residence was a large white

painted adobe house which was located on a big grassy knoll and because of its location could be seen from all sides for miles away. It was one of the many famous spots in the great Sulphur Springs Valley. The adobe brick house was composed of eight large rooms, four on each side of the large hall open at each end and running clear through the middle of the structure. In the south four rooms were located the kitchen, dining room and the bunkhouse quarters for the many cowhands. On the other side were the office, sitting room and two bedrooms. This was Uncle Jimmy's side of the house.

The spring roundup was starting and was to work north as far as the Chiricahua Cattle Company's southern line, then turn south to work the east side of the valley lying alongside the Swisshelm Range to the east; then down the valley as far south as the Mexican border; (there was no Douglas, Arizona, at that time) then north again to the 4-Bar headquarters. As most of the saddle horses had been running out all winter many had not been ridden since the fall roundup the year before; the horses were all fat and some of them rearing to go. As many of the horses will buck when they have not been ridden for several months we were all watching to see the fun as the boys mounted their horses.

Albert Cole who was working for Jake Shearer, owner of the Double Rod outfit, had been having some trouble getting a little brown horse saddled and we could easily see that Cole's horse was going to buck. Uncle Jimmy had joined the bunch watching to see what the little brown horse would do. One of the boys eared the horse's head down and Cole vaunted into the saddle; instead of a quirt Cole had in his hand a leather strap about sixteen or eighteen inches long. The horse started bucking straight down the hill, Cole seemed to be doing all right using the strap for a quirt. I do not know yet just how the little brown unloaded Cole, but to us it looked as if he turned a back somersault off the horse, landing on his feet at the rear of the horse and when he landed the momentum of his body caused Cole to bring the strap down on the brown's rump. At this Uncle Jimmy exploded; "By Gad!" said he, "He never quit hitting him, did he?" Everyone except Cole, of course, appreciated this example of Uncle Jimmy's wit.

Before we had gathered our first trainload of Erie Cattle we were joined by a Mr. Stubb Shattuck, one of the owners from the East. I will never forget the first morning after the arrival of Shattuck. The guest room on the ground floor east window opened out in the yard and was about twenty-five feet away from where the chuck wagon was spotted and the cook, a noted character called "Shoot-em-Up Dick" (I never knew Dick's real name) had his fire going and was busy getting breakfast. Stubb Shattuck, finding no water in the pitcher which was set in a wash bowl in his room, poked his head out the window and calling to Dick, said, "Oh! I say, servant, will you get me a little water, please." Dick looked around and said, "Get it yourself, you old bald-headed son of a b—, if you want any water." Shattuck pretty nearly broke his neck pulling his head back in from the window. I got well acquainted with Mr. Shattuck for he worked the drag end with me while trailing the cattle to be shipped at Willcox and Stubb said, "You know, Dick's answer to me that morning was the best thing that could have happened for I quickly sensed that I had a different brand of men to deal with than those who would be servants."

While in Willcox with our first trainload an amusing incident took place which lingers in my memories of the early West. It was about the year 1920 before ladies were accepted riding straddle; the convenience of wearing pants and riding with both feet in the stirrups had been proven years before and was permitted and accepted as correct on most western ranches. But when riding to town it was still proper to ride sidesaddle because of the criticism which was sure to come if this custom was not followed.

Willcox, Arizona was surrounded on all sides by different ranches completely devoted to the raising of beef cattle, for there were no farms surrounding the town at that time. One day a young lady from a local ranch, located at the north end of the Chiricahua Mountains in a valley lying between the Chiricahuas and the Dos Cabezas Mountains to the north, made a trip from the ranch to Willcox. She used an ordinary western stock saddle with its horn instead of a regular side saddle but she did have on her sidesaddle riding skirt. She rode straddle until approaching the town; then she threw her right leg over and around the saddle horn and she was in a perfect sidesaddle position.

She rode up to a hitching rack in front of De Soto's general store, slipped her leg over the horn and dismounted. But something went wrong—the riding habit instead of coming free caught on the horn and pulled the skirt almost over her head leaving the central part of her body very much exposed. A drunken cowhand passing by at this moment rushed up to help; seeing her rear exposed he thought only of covering her with something. Jerking off his Stetson he slapped it over her rear, noticed that it did not cover everything, so turned and called to the crowd on the sidewalk, "More hat! More hat." The lady was rescued from her position and for years created a smile whenever one thought of her embarrassing moment when one hat was not enough to cover.

While we were still in Willcox waiting for railroad cars for the cattle I was told of the mistreatment of a poor old Chinaman. In earlier days many mining camps were not very kind to the sons of China. For years some camps kept posted a sign reading something like this: "Chinaman, do not let the sun go down on you in this camp—get out of town before the sun goes down." The feeling was not so much against the individual as against the type of business in which the Chinaman was usually engaged. They mostly were found running a restaurant or a laundry. As miners were constantly being killed in the mines, many widows could make their living by running a boarding house or a home laundry, so the camps wanted to preserve these two ways by which a miner's widow could make her living; hence the ban on all Chinamen. This often caused cowpunchers as well as miners to declare an open season on the sons of China.

I heard that Grant Wheeler, a cowboy who afterward joined with Joe George and staged a train holdup, was riding down the main street in Willcox, when he observed a Chinaman hurrying down the sidewalk; Grant jumped his horse in on the sidewalk and cut the Chinaman out into the open street, at the same time building a loop in his rope, which was tied hard and fast to the saddle horn for Grant was a tied-rope man. The Chinaman, seeing that Grant was going to rope him, ran up and put his arms around a hitching post thinking this would save him. Grant roped Chinaman, post and all, and hit the end of the rope at full speed. The rope broke but it drew the Chinaman into a perfect figure eight, the poor soul collapsing as soon as the rope slackened around his middle.

This will give you some idea of how the poor Chink was treated; yet, never had a Chinaman fought back in such an ordeal until one day in Tombstone where

The Back-Down of Butch Cassidy

Prominent in the crew working for the Erie Cattle
Company were Jim James, Andy Darnell, Frank Johnson,
Bob Johnson, Irwin Bradshaw, Emery Cooper, Perry
Tucker and two newcomers, Jim Lowe and Will Mc-
Ginnis. Perry Tucker was a top hand and was often used
as a straw boss by Bob Johnson, the superintendent. One
day the mail brought a letter to Tucker from Captain
French, his old employer, in which he pleaded with Perry
to return at once to his old job, saying, "I really need
you." Tucker left in a day or two to join his old outfit in
Alma, New Mexico. While with the Erie Cattle Company
Tucker had formed a friendship with Jim Lowe and
McGinnis, so it was no surprise to us when Lowe received
a letter from Tucker asking him to recruit several

cowhands from the old bunch and report to him at Alma at the earliest convenience. Lowe talked with several of us; and as a result Clay McGonegal, Jim James and myself agreed to go to Alma and work for Perry. With Lowe and McGinnis added, five of us made the trip north. It took us about four days to go overland to Alma, New Mexico. We all reported to Perry and that night he filled us in on why he needed an outside bunch of riders whom he could depend upon.

It seems that Captain French's range boss was making no attempt to protect the Captain's interest, resulting in a wholesale stealing of the W S calves by a group of small owners who were also running their spreads on the W S range. The W S range was located on the headwaters of the Frisco River and was well supplied with grass and water. This was mostly open government range with the only land holdings of Captain French being on several hundred acres of bottom land, on which he had built his headquarters residence surrounded by fields of alfalfa from which he put up hay to take care of what feeding was necessary throughout the winter months. As the climate was usually not very severe, feeding was necessary only for the few poor cows which always show up on any southwest cow range and the Hereford bulls which were usually taken in about the middle of September and fed throughout the winter months.

The old foreman had been discharged and we arrived a few days before the fall roundup started. On our first roundup thrown together, we found several large calves following W S cows with the brands of the little owners on them. We rebranded these calves with the W S iron and barred out the other brands thereon. This rebranding almost caused trouble, but with Tucker backed up by the five of us from Arizona, all of us armed and ready for business, trouble was averted. After the first roundup, the little cowmen left only two of their men to work with our outfit and made an attempt to round up the range ahead of us. As cattle being driven in to the roundup ground always kick up considerable dust, we quickly spotted the attempt to round up ahead of us, resulting in our dropping our own work and riding fast. We were able to reach their roundup ground just as they got the cattle together. We rode up at this moment and Tucker in the lead said, "Thanks, boys, for getting them together; we will take over now and do our job." Again there was much muttering and they rode off to one side to talk things over for a few moments and then took off. We barred out about eighty calves from this roundup. As Captain French, who was rather an old man, never rode himself, it is easily seen that if his foreman had stayed on and the cattle run out through the winter the boys would have made a nice cleanup of big calves. Altogether we barred out about three hundred calves in this fall work. In the meantime Perry told me confidentially that Jim Lowe was the celebrated Wyoming outlaw, Butch Cassidy.

The following spring Captain French sold out the range cattle to a Montana outfit and the cattle had to be trailed to Magdalena, Socorro County, New Mexico, and from there shipped by rail to their destination in the north country. Our first trail herd consisted of about sixteen hundred head of mixed cattle, cows and calves, steers and bulls. Jim Lowe, or Butch Cassidy as he was known only to Perry and myself and his pardner McGinnis, was made boss of the trail herd. As this trail was to be several days long and to most of us the country was unknown, the two lead men had to be men familiar with the trail. We had two men in our outfit—Joe Champion and a cowhand we all called by his nickname, Black River, because of his home range being somewhere cattle strung out perfectly. Cassidy again (only I knew he was Butch Cassidy—to all the others he was Jim Lowe) rode up at this moment and asked what was the matter. Black River immediately jumped him, "What's the matter! What the hell's the matter with you, turning these cattle back at the foot of the hill. If you don't know your business, you have no damned business being a trail boss." Black River had walked out a few feet in front of us and was facing Cassidy. Cassidy, seeing that he had made a mistake in having the cattle stopped, replied that he did not know the country. Black River told him at this point that he was a damn poor man to put in charge of a trail herd. I could see Cassidy's eyes blazing but he kept his head: I fully expected to see Cassidy gun Black River down. Instead he apologized to the boys, told Black River and Champion, "From now on, as you know the trail, you handle the head end." After some hard work we got the cattle strung out and up and over the hill. From then on it was smooth trailing over the San Augustine plains.

That evening Cassidy came over and talked to me for several minutes. I told Butch I fully expected him to take Black River on. "No," Butch said, "I realized I was in the wrong, so I took it." Having seen Cassidy pull and shoot, I am certain that Black River can thank his lucky stars that Cassidy had a sense of justice. Black River would never have had a chance. I also had a lot of respect after that for Butch Cassidy as a man. He could easily have disposed of Black River, but realizing he was in the wrong, he took Black River's abuse, and saved the morale of the crew.

One Wild Night in Alma, New Mexico

But I can not pass on without the story of one wild night in Alma. The night before we were to start on the trail to Magdalena with Captain French's herd of range cattle, Alma was giving a dance, one of the usual weekly hoe-downs for which the West was so famous. Here were danced the old waltzes, two-steps, schottisches, and of course the most famous of all, the square dance. Alma consisted of one general store, Coates and Roe, with a bar in the back room, the dance hall and Little Johnny Ward's saloon adjoining the dance hall. Early arrivals soon found that it would be a big dance, for many were already there and more coming.

There was still a good deal of bad feeling toward Captain French's outfit even if the Captain was quitting the range to avoid any trouble. Episodes of many years past with the W S outfit were still fresh in some memories and, in particular, what we'll call the "little men" still were smarting under the defeat of their plans by Perry Tucker and the boys from Arizona. So tonight we had to be careful, for even a parlor match struck at the right moment could be the means of starting trouble. So when McGinnis, Black River, Clay McGonegal, Jim James and I were riding down from the ranch on our way to the dance McGinnis called our attention to the situation and cautioned us all to be on our good behavior. He asked me not to take a drink of any kind in order to be able to help him keep the boys out of trouble. We had only one dangerous man in our outfit. He was a man who would not fight but was a great bluffer and he could bluff so well that he had several times almost got in trouble, only getting out by backing down at the last moment. If a man had the guts to go against James and call him, he need never again question his nerve for James would stay with you even to going after your gun and quitting only at the last moment. As McGonegal and I were very close friends, I asked him to go slow on the drinking.

There were so many at the dance that it was necessary to issue numbers, the even numbers to dance first, followed by the dancers holding the odd numbers. James of course took on several drinks and as he did not dance spent most of his time in little Johnny Ward's place, sitting at one of the card tables. There was also another Johnny Ward, known as Big Johnny Ward, but they had no relation to each other, however. Big Johnny Ward was one of the little men whose calves had been rebranded and his brand barred out when found following W S cows; he had a little chip on his shoulder on account of this and did not have much liking for any of the W S cowhands.

The night was dark as pitch—one could not see another person outside unless he was caught in the glare from the dance hall or Little Johnny Ward's place. I was standing in the doorway of Coates and Roe's store, having just given McGonegal a talking-to over his drinking too much. Clay said he was only drinking port wine and had not taken a drink of whiskey. Anyway port wine or not, McGonegal was getting drunk and noisy and I had been trying to get him to slow down. At this moment I heard James somewhere out in the dark tell someone to cut his wolf loose. I ran as fast as I could in the direction of James' voice, closed in on him and happened to be lucky enough to get my hands on his gun. At the same time I called out to whoever was facing James to go slow, that I would handle him. In the struggle to get James' gun away from him we wrestled out into the glare from the dance hall windows. McGinnis had reached me by then, James had such a grip on the gun that I could not break his hold, so I hung on to his gun with my left hand and brought him down with a crack over the head with the 45 which I had pulled for this purpose. I took James' gun and then turned to find out who he was having trouble with. It was Big Johnny Ward. Ward stated that he had gone into the saloon and seeing James sitting at the table and noticing he had not been dancing wondered if James had a number. He asked James what number he had, to which he replied he had 44, throwing his hand to his gun at the same time. Big Johnny walked over to the bar saying, "Give me my gun, a 45, a little larger gun than yours and I think it will do me." James had turned and walked outside; Big Johnny followed resulting in James telling him to turn his wolf loose. It was then that I came into the picture. James can thank his stars that Ward could not see in the darkness that he had his gun out for Ward would surely have dropped him; in fact Ward said he could not see James at all. Well, we got James settled down, the fact that I had hit him with my gun sobered him somewhat. James always leaned on me to help him and had a lot of respect for my friendship but he felt that maybe he had lost that friendship and that also had its sobering effect on him.

By this time I could hear McGonegal raising hell over at Coates and Roe. I told James that I wanted him to go back to the ranch and would try to get McGonegal to go along. Knowing that I could never command McGonegal to come with me to the ranch I had to figure out a way that he would go along with. I went in to Coates and Roe's and calling to Clay to come outside told him that James had made a gun play and we had to get him out but refused to go unless Clay would go with him. Clay agreed that we would have to get James out of there so we went to get our horses. Black River agreed to go with us, so I told him to get James and I would bring the horses. As we passed the dance hall McGonegal tried to ride his horse inside but McGinnis stopped him; I arrived at this moment and took charge and the four of us started for the ranch. McGonegal had made me promise that he and I would return to the dance after getting James safely to the ranch. Before we reached the outside gates to the ranch McGonegal had broken away and tried to dodge Black River and me and get back to Alma. I told Black River to tie the gate with his rope so if McGonegal got away the tied gate would stop him and enable us to get him before he escaped.

Inside the gate the road passed through one of the alfalfa fields; the hay had been cut and put up so the ground was as smooth as a floor. By this time the moon had risen and the field was bathed in clear moonlight. When McGonegal saw the field he immediately broke away, with the three of us after him; he suddenly jumped off his horse and said he had lost his gun and commenced to search for it on foot. I jumped off and joined him and motioned to Black River and James to take our horses and pull for the house. This left McGonegal and me on foot; Clay asked about the horses and I told him we would find them at the barn. McGonegal kept searching as if looking for the gun; I caught a glimpse of his eyes at the time, and from the gleam in them I felt sure he either had the gun or had never lost it in the first place. I stepped up alongside of him, lifted his coat and pulled the gun from his waistband. He told me that he had always considered me his best friend but by this act I had proven otherwise; said I had promised him we would go back as soon as we got James safely to the ranch. I told Clay the horses were up at the barn so let's go get them. When we arrived at the wagon we found McGonegal's bed and with Black River helping me we threw him down and pulled off his boots and hid them. I quickly got my horse and rode to join McGinnis to help him ride herd on the boys still left in Alma. As I rode off I could still hear Clay saying he always thought we were good friends.

I got back to Alma and joined McGinnis; nothing further happened but I will always remember that wild night in Alma. I left with the trail herd the next morning; McGonegal later returned to Arizona; whatever became of James I do not know. McGinnis later took up with the Ketchum gang of train robbers and was captured and sent to prison.

The Road of No Return

Shortly after getting the trail herd to the railroad in Magdalena, I left the employ of Captain French to return to Arizona. There I joined Tuck Potter, helping him get started with a ranch in Dixie Canyon, which was on the east slope of the Mule Mountains and the west side of Sulphur Springs Valley in Cochise County, Arizona Territory. Arizona was still a territory and did not join the states until the year 1912.

It was Potter's intention to make a ranch out of this place which he had chosen in Dixie Canyon and I was helping him with the chores. A year or two later Tuck and his wife built a road up to his chosen spot and resided there for several years. But Potter was not married at the time of this story. We had run short of a few essentials, such as flour, baking powder, beans, bacon and spuds, and Tuck had left early that morning, leading a pack horse, on his way into Bisbee to get the needed supplies. The route into town took him about two miles south along the foothills of the Mules, and then west up a canyon which joined the head of Brewery Gulch, one of the main streets of Bisbee at that time. The total distance was about eight miles.

I busied myself about the place, tightened up the wire around the horse corral, dragged in some wood from the canyon and did-the essential things so necessary in a camp of this kind. We had no house, using a tent for our sleeping quarters and cooking on an open fire located a few feet in front of the tent. We hobbled our horses up the canyon to keep them from straying off, fed a small feed of rolled barley to the others whenever they came in to camp, and in this way avoided the usual trouble with horses in an open camp of this nature. The day passed quickly, I had built up a fire, put on the Dutch oven to heat up, getting ready to prepare a quick meal for Potter when he returned. Darkness fell and no Potter. I cooked up a snack for myself and wondered what had happened to Tuck.

The next morning I caught up one of the horses; I had kept up a night horse as we always did; I rode the night horse up the canyon a ways, caught one of the hobbled horses, changed on to him, hobbling the night horse with the bunch and rode back to camp. It was still rather early but Potter had had plenty of time to make it back to camp even if he had found it necessary to stay in Bisbee over night. I was commencing to be rather worried. Tuck had had trouble with Tom Hudspeth who operated a saloon in Brewery Gulch and Potter had to ride right by Hudspeth's place on his way down Brewery Gulch to the town's center. The more I thought about this, the more worried I became, and when ten o'clock had arrived I stepped up on my horse and headed for Bisbee.

Arriving at the head of Brewery Gulch I rode down carefully by Hudspeth's place; it was too early for anyone to be up, for this was the redlight district—no one was in sight, so I continued my way down the canyon to the main part of Bisbee. I could tell the moment I rode on to the main street that something out of the ordinary had happened, the narrow streets and sidewalks were thronged with an unusually large number of miners for this time of day. I spotted a man I knew in the crowd, rode up to him and asked what had happened, asking in almost the same breath if he had seen Potter. "You haven't heard the news, Axford?" "Potter is probably down at Naco; the Mexicans have arrested Joe Rhodes and Jim Herrin and have them in jail on the Mexican side; it is reported that they intend to make an example of them and that they are to be shot. All the cowmen in this country are assembling at Naco and are going to rescue Rhodes and Herrin." Without getting off my horse at all in Bisbee, I headed down the canyon towards Naco which was nine miles south and straddled the international boundary line between the towns of Naco, Arizona, and Naco, Mexico. About a half hour later I arrived at Naco and found thirty-five cattlemen and cowpunchers congregated in Clint Hudspeth's saloon, and Potter was among them. Clint was a brother of Tom with whom Tuck had had trouble, but Clint and Potter were good friends.

As stated before, the town of Naco is really two towns, one American and one Mexican, with the international line running east and west between the two towns. The railroad which ran from Benson to Bisbee ran a spur east and west, also alongside the boundary line and between the two towns. When I arrived at Hudspeth's place a meeting was in progress, the boys were receiving a report from Babe Thompson who was foreman of the Turkey Track Cattle Company owned by W. C. Greene, B. A. Packard and Babe Thompson; the Turkey Track holdings were all located south of Naco in Mexican territory. Thompson's report was that the Mexicans were going to start with Rhodes and Herrin for Arispe the next morning. As the Mexicans were noted for taking advantage of a fugitive law under which they often shot the prisoners at a given spot, claiming that they had tried to get away, the boys were really worried. They discussed this problem thoroughly and figured that something must be done at once. The Mexicans noticing that a large number of cattlemen had congregated in Naco and evidently aware that an attempt to rescue the prisoners might be made, had sent a courier to Colonel Kosterlitzsky who commanded the Mexican Rurales, or rangers, asking for help. Kosterlitzsky had arrived during the early morning with about a hundred of his rangers.

At each end of the Mexican street which faced the American side was an adobe house in course of construction with about two to three feet of the foundations laid. Kosterlitzsky had posted a part of his men in these two houses and in this way could control almost any movement made to rescue the prisoners from the American side. After considerable discussion as to ways and means to accomplish their purpose it was decided by the boys that King, who was a pardner of Rhodes, should pick one man out of the bunch to ride with him. The others were to crawl up to the railroad grade which was about three feet above the ground level and would thus afford good protection; then when all were in position, to open fire on Kosterlitzsky's men, driving them off the street, and at a given signal King and his pardner were to come riding out from behind the Hudspeth place equipped with an axe apiece and their six-shooters. Under cover of the boys at the railroad grade they were to ride straight through to the jail, use the axes to chop down the jail's wooden door and taking Rhodes and Herrin on behind, were to return to the American side.

The thought came to me at this moment that this would be a suicide ride; whoever was chosen to make the trip would not be coming back—the odds were too great. King looked us over, then quietly said, "I will choose Axford." This was a double surprise to me; while I knew King, still I was not what you would call a close friend and I felt certain that someone closer to him would be picked. Anyway it was now up to me. I had no thought of refusing to go. King and I went outside to get the axes—both were supplied from Hudspeth's woodshed. Our horses were saddled, the boys were already crawling towards the railroad, when with a loud clatter and in a cloud of dust, a troop of cavalry from Fort Huachuca arrived at full gallop.

It seems that someone had wired the President that trouble was about to start between American citizens and Mexicans and that something had to be done and done quickly to avoid the start of war between the two countries. The troops were colored, belonging to the famous Ninth Cavalry which had been of great help to the Rough Riders in the Spanish-American War. The Captain in charge immediately took over, the boys were called back from the railroad grade and King and I were left standing by, ready to go.

It has been said that a couple of cavalry colored troopers in trying to cross the international line into Naco, Mexico, were challenged by the sentry with "No pasa la linea"; turning to an American standing by he asked, "What does he say?" "Not to pass the line." "No boss, we'se not going to pass the line, but if Uncle Sam tells us to take that line and pack it way down into Mexico, we's gwine to do just that."

Many years passed between that event and this story, and that fact that I lived to tell the tale can be credited to the prompt arrival of the famous Ninth Cavalry. But for all those years, I always shuddered a little when I thought of how close King and I were to the road of no return.

When You Are Your Own Judge

While riding over the Swisshelm Mountain country, I found where considerable work had been done by early day miners on some showings of copper ore. I interested C. L. Cummings of Tombstone and Ed Jacklin, who with Cummings owned the 7-D brand of cattle running then in Sulphur Springs Valley. We decided to take a try at a little mining, and one day when getting our camp outfit together, blacksmith tools, and the like, a man by the name of Mowbry came riding by and joined us in the work. Charlie Mowbry was of Swedish descent, stood about six feet one in his stocking feet and was considered one of the best, if not the best, of the single or double jack miners in the Southwest. Jacklin was to furnish the camp and mining supplies and one man to work opposite me while doing the mining. We worked a while before dinner getting our outfit together, Mowbry of course helping, when we went in to get dinner ready, and this was a job we all pitched in on. Jacklin asked Mowbry if he wanted a job, explained that he would have to break me in to use a single jack hammer, as I was a green kid and knew nothing about mining work, and also how to handle dynamite. Mowbry agreed to work, wages were settled and Mowbry hired on the spot. Old Ed called me to one side, told me that Mowbry was considered one of the best hard rock miners in the country and how lucky it was for us that Charlie dropped in.

We moved our supplies to the east slope of the Swisshelms and established our camp; setting up the blacksmith shop was Jacklin's work—Ed had been a blacksmith at the Toughnut Mine in Tombstone in the earlier days and knew the blacksmith business. We picked out what we considered the best spot to work; here was about a four-inch streak of copper glance ore; this streak of ore was in the middle of a garnet conglomeration and where it did not show a foot wall, the hanging wall was plainly in evidence. A single jack hammer is always either three-and-a-half or four pounds in weight, the double jacks were eight-pound hammers. As Mowbry prided himself on his great strength—the single jacks weighed four pounds—Charlie would not use the sissy three-and-a-half pound hammer.

As soon as camp was established and the place to work chosen, Jacklin went back to his ranch and Mowbry and I were on our way. After three months work we were in and down about seventy-five feet, having followed the hanging wall with a tunnel thirty feet straight in, on the level to where the hanging wall took about a 70 degree dip, then down another forty-five feet, the rich streak of copper glance quitting where the ledge or deposit started its dip. What a man Mowbry proved to be! He could take the eight-pound hammer when drilling and make me lay the four-pound hammer down before he would—he was that strong! We ran into some blue limestone on the foot-wall side of our work; this, of course, called for the heavier hammer so I had to turn the drills while Charlie did the double jack work. At first I was a little afraid that Mowbry might miss the head of the drill but I soon learned that Charlie never missed—he was a wonderful hammerman.

During the three months we had been working together I had learned to love this great hulk of a man, always agreeable—who joined with the cooking and camp duties and was just a wonderful all-around guy. What I did not know about Charlie was that he was a periodical drinker. The three months he had worked steadily had built up a stake and Charlie intended to do something about it. One morning, he served notice that he wanted to go into Bisbee and told me he intended to be gone about eight days and that if he failed to get back in that time I was to ride in after him. Mowbry had a nice, double rigged saddle outfit and a very good-looking horse about eight years old; altogether the horse and outfit were easily worth one hundred and twenty-five dollars. Well, Charlie left for Bisbee. I had given him an order on Jacklin for his wages which amounted to two hundred and twenty-five dollars; Jacklin was paying him two fifty a day and his board. So Charlie was worth, counting the horse and saddle, about three hundred and fifty dollars. I had to remain in camp in order to protect our camp and supplies.

Well, the eight days passed and no Mowbry; I waited two days more, then saddled up and rode in after Charlie.

I found him up Brewery Gulch drinking heavily and told him I wanted him to come back to camp. He said he would go if I would get his horse from the livery stable. I agreed to this and, leading the horse, rode up Brewery Gulch after Charlie. I finally got him in the saddle and we started to leave town. Where the gulch joined the main street, he broke away and started a run right through the middle of the town; I raced after him, caught the bridle away from him and thought I could get him out of town by leading his horse. This might have worked if I had tied him on, but when we reached the junction of Brewery Gulch, Charlie jumped off the horse and started to run up the canyon. I finally stopped him and seeing that he was not through with his vacation, told him I would take his horse back to the stable and for him to return when he was through with his drinking. This he promised to do.

I returned to camp and was getting ready to ride to the ranch to ask Jacklin to get another man when Charlie came walking in; this was about noon. Well, I have seen some hard-looking characters in my time but I believe Charlie was in the worst condition of all of them. Here was a great big, handsome man, completely down and out, dirty, hair uncombed, eyes bloodshot, clothes filthy. One could hardly believe that a man could so degrade himself in such a short period of time. Well, I got Charlie fed, he took a bath and changed clothes and looked some better. "Charlie", I said, "evidently you have left your horse in Bisbee. I will ride in and bring him out for you." "No need to," said Charlie, "I sold the horse and saddle for seventy-five dollars. I walked all the way from Bisbee."

The Erie Cattle Company had an old pack horse named Smuggler. Smuggler had been a top cow horse in his day but for several years had been reduced to being a pack horse used by the boys when camping out around the range while looking for any unbranded calves which the roundup had missed. Incidentally, if the fall work finds eighty percent of the cattle when rounding up it is called a clean roundup. These unbranded calves of course have to be sought out and branded. Usually two boys, taking a range tent, grub and the like, start camping around the range at the different springs or water troughs and must rope and brand the calves on the open range. As the boys will be moving camp often, it is necessary to add a pack horse or two to the string of horses, in order to move. Old Smuggler was a favorite pack horse—he was gentle and easily caught. It is seldom you can find a horse that will let you walk up to him when running out with other horses on the open range. Smuggler was one that would—you could catch him anytime, anywhere.

Mowbry, in walking from Bisbee, had reached the center of Sulphur Springs Valley just above the old Copper Queen Ranch. Charlie was tired and sore from the long walk; this was somewhat short of half way—he still had about ten miles to go. He recognized Old Smuggler with a bunch of horses and knowing that he was easy to catch, walked over to the horses and easily caught him. He had no rope, but managed to tear up in strips a large bandanna handkerchief and made a string long enough to control the horse, for Smuggler was very gentle. Charlie said the muscles in his legs and especially at his hip joints were so sore that he had to walk slowly, one step at a time, always accompanied by considerable pain. He stood looking at the horse for several minutes, then talking to himself, said, "Mowbry, you had a good horse and saddle and over two hundred dollars when you went to Bisbee. You have lost it all—you do not deserve to ride." So, turning Smuggler loose, he started the long ten-mile walk to the mine. Here was a man who stood for those few moments and reviewed the evidence, then passed judgment on himself. Charlie walked.

We later sold our mining claims for forty thousand dollars, getting ten percent down and no further payments were made, the company of inexperienced miners quitting after several months of work.

While I was mining in the Swisshelms, the Ketchum gang of trainrobbers came into the Arizona territory. The band consisted of four men, Tom Ketchum, Sam Ketchum, his brother, Will Carver and Dave Aikens. They made a camp somewhere south of what at one time was the ranch of Buckskin Frank Leslie, one of early day Tombstone's celebrated gunmen. From this camp they boldly rode to the different ranches in the vicinity where, if not exactly welcomed, they were tolerated. In those days a rancher had no protection from the sheriff's office, there were no means of rapid communication or transportation except the horse.

The band often came to the camp which Mowbry and I had established in the Swisshelms and bought groceries if we had them to spare, and sometimes cartridges for their six-shooters, as all were carrying single-action Colt 45's. We had no cartridges for the rifles they were carrying—box magazine, 30-40 Winchester's—powerful guns, easily outshooting the 30-30's that most ranchers used, and the first guns of this caliber we had ever seen. One day Dave Aikens, who I believe was part Comanche Indian, came into camp and stated he had left the Ketchum gang on account of trouble he had with Tom Ketchum. For a week or ten days he made a camp somewhere east of my camp, usually paying us a visit each evening when he would join us around our campfire.

What he told me about Tom Ketchum convinced me that Tom was a cold-blooded murderer and a very brutal man. Tom's brother Sam Ketchum, Aikens said, was as fine a man as could be and he also had a good word for Will Carver. When Aikens left the country on his way north I rode with him a few miles, turning back about midnight and wishing him the best of luck in his intended efforts to go straight from here on. I received one letter from him from Idaho and never heard from him again. I am sure he turned out to be a good law-abiding citizen. He had the quality to make it that way.

I must also tell you about Bill Lutely, an Englishman owning a little cowspread in the valley lying east of the Swisshelm Mountains where I was mining. Lutely's brand was the Bar Boot, a bar just above the figure of a boot on the left side of the animal. It was during the war between the British and the Boers in South Africa. As I always tried to keep posted on what was going on in the world, I was very welcome to stop over night at any of the ranches and especially at Lutely's. The war had been running against the British, Ladysmith was besieged, Mafeking had been taken and the Boers had the British Army on the run. I had stayed overnight a couple of times during the early part of the war and of course, as my sympathy lay with the Boers, had all the best of the hot arguments which Lutely and I always held, after the supper dishes had been washed and put away.

Finally things commenced to get very much better for the British forces, they stopped hurling their forces against the Boers, entrenched positions, took to by-passing the Boers, relieved Ladysmith and retook Mafeking, and the arguments were all in favor of the British—in fact they were winning the war. The last time I had stayed overnight with Lutely I had all the best of the argument. It was about four in the afternoon, I was on my way to Bisbee and had to pass by Lutely's place; I had a choice of staying all night with Lutely or of riding on several miles further and spending the night with Jim Hunasaker. Lutely could see me coming when I was about a quarter of a mile away. I saw Bill rush out to the fence and open the gate, waiting for me to ride in. I could tell how eager he was to have me stay by the quick way he walked from the house to open the gate. I knew that this time Lutely would have the best of all the arguments, so I decided to ride on down and stay with Hunasaker. Bill was standing holding the gate open when he saw I had no intention of stopping. He dropped the gate and followed me down the fence for a ways, shaking his fist at me, telling me at the same time that I always stopped when I had the best of it but this time when "I have got you where I want you, you refuse to stop." I laughed at him but kept on riding. I have heard Lutely say many times that Axford is a wonder when he has all the best of it, but will not meet you when you have the nod. Anyway, I will always remember Bill Lutely as one of my good friends, a perfect gentleman and a good scout.

and also owned a large part of the town, was one of the doctor's bondsmen. The hospital, including the poor house, usually had about eighty-five inmates.

As this was in about the year 1900, experienced or trained personnel to staff the hospital were few and far between. The steward in charge of the hospital was unsatisfactory to Dr. Bacon and he was looking for a suitable man to replace him. When talking to his bondsmen about his need for another steward, Dr. Bacon made the remark that if he could get hold of a good young man he would train him himself, taking his time to give him the training necessary. Cummings said he thought he had just the young man the doctor needed. Said he was out on a ranch with Cummings' ranch pardner, Ed Jacklin, and would have him brought in so the doctor could look him over. I was brought in and under Bacon's supervision was taught the many things necessary and soon was in full charge of the hospital and its eighty-five inmates.

As the hospital was about three-quarters of a mile west of Tombstone, the local stage would bring the new patients right to the hospital. When a new patient arrived it was necessary for me to call Dr. Bacon at once, describing the case, which often called for immediate surgery. One day the stage brought in a young man named Albert Cole who had both of his hands wrapped in bandages. I saw at once that the Doctor should look at Cole as soon as possible and phoned Bacon giving him the particulars of the case as I saw them. Bacon soon arrived bringing a Dr. Bedford with him. Cole was taken into the surgery, the bandages on his hands removed showing both hands with badly swollen joints and large blotches over most of the hands and fingers. I noticed the exchange of looks between the two doctors immediately after one of the swollen joints had been lanced. Bacon, who had done the lancing, immediately went to the wash bowl and pouring in a strong antiseptic, in addition to scouring his hands thoroughly, let them remain in the solution or several minutes, then rinsed them in alcohol.

Noticing the extra precautions taken by Bacon and the looks exchanged between the two doctors, I realized that here was a dangerous case. Bacon handed me a pair of rubber gloves to be put on before we rebandaged Cole's hands, told me to thoroughly sterilize my hands when through and to burn the gloves at once. When the two doctors left the surgery I followed them outside, stopped them and told them I was convinced from the way they had acted that Cole had a case of leprosy. Both doctors placed a finger on their mouths and whispering to me advised me to isolate Cole and not to breathe a word of this to anyone for if it got out they would not have a patient left in the hospital. In the meantime, they would try to figure out just what to do. I had known Cole for some time, having worked cattle with him in Sulphur Springs Valley, and had a great deal of sympathy for him. The actions of the doctors has also aroused Cole's suspicions and when I returned to the room to finish bandaging his hands he wanted to know what his trouble was. I told Cole that in the doctor's opinions he had leprosy. When I finished bandaging, Cole told me that if I would give him a pair of shoes and a couple of dollars he would be in Old Mexico by morning as the line was only about twenty miles away. I gave Cole a pair of my shoes and five dollars cash. When the doctors came down the next morning the first question asked was concerning Cole's condition. I had not advised the doctors of what I had done so when I answered that Cole was gone, it came as a complete surprise. They finally got the story from me and as they left after their morning checkup, Bacon was heard to remark to Bedford that he thought he would have to give me a raise.

Some of you oldtimers will remember the famous case of General Waddell who, having a case of leprosy several years later, was shunted between California and Arizona several times because neither state would accept him. Albert Cole's sister was the wife of General Waddell. Whatever happened to Albert Cole is still unknown. He no doubt made it to Old Mexico. The handling of this case may not have been exactly legal, but it was very effective.

I seemed to fit into this job in the hospital and was soon able to tell a case of pneumonia or typhoid fever as soon as I looked at the patient. About this time Dr. Bacon sent down an Italian about 45 years of age who had a touch of lumbago in his back. We had a hot air machine which was used in cases requiring heat. Bacon's note told me to hook the hot air machine to his back, this being done by backing him up to the machine on a stool and tying him in with cloth wings which were attached, and to leave him in until he complained, then to release him and drench him down with a handful or two of alcohol. I was to charge him a dollar and a half for each treatment and I could keep it for my trouble.

I hooked the Italian in and started the machine. I was immediately called out in the yard to separate two oldtimers who had got into a fight over their part of the cleaning up job, which all able inmates of the place were required to do since the hospital was also a poor farm. One of the old men had a badly damaged eye and I took him into the operating room in order to give his eye attention. This all took several minutes and in the meantime I had completely forgotten the hot-air patient. As soon as I thought of him I rushed to the dispensary where he was sitting, found him limp as a dishrag and covered with perspiration. I unfastened him immediately, grabbed up a double handful of alcohol and dashed it on him. An examination of the thermometer which registered somewhere around 600 degrees showed it to be broken, whether from the extreme heat or what I will never know. A couple of days later Dr. Bacon asked me how my hot air patient was coming along. I told him I didn't know, that the one treatment evidently was enough, for he never came back.

Another case in which I played a part took place about a year after I had taken charge at the hospital. Joe Burgano, an Italian miner, had just been rushed to the hospital with a badly fractured skull. Burgano, while working in a mine in the Black Diamond Mining district in the Dragoon Mountains, had been struck in the right temple by a rock which had been carelessly dropped by the man taking a car off the mine cage on the surface. The mine was owned by a group of local citizens among which Paul Warnekros, owner of one of Tombstone's largest stores, was the largest stockholder. Warnekros had accompanied the rig which brought Burgano in to the hospital and impressed on me that an immediate operation was necessary not only to save the patient's life but was doubly necessary, for if Burgano should die the damages that would have to be paid would break them all.

Dr. Bacon had gone to New York to take another postgraduate course and before leaving had arranged for a young M.D., a pharmacist whom I'll call Jones, to make a trip to the hospital to protect his bondsmen. He told me that Jones was a licensed physician, but not a surgeon. Should an occasion arise that would call for surgery, Bacon had made arrangements with a Dr. Wallace who was spending a vacation in Tombstone at the time; further he had made arrangements with Dr. Caven in Bisbee to assist Wallace if necessary.

I placed Burgano in the surgical ward and gave the necessary first aid. Upon removing the bandage which was around the wound, I found a badly fractured skull, with a number of shattered bone pieces showing in the brain material which was already oozing out of the wound. Realizing that this did indeed call for an immediate operation, I hastily replaced the bandages with fresh ones, saw to the sterilizing of the tools necessary to do the operation and tried to reach Wallace on the phone. I was advised that Dr. Wallace had left early that morning on a picnic trip to Cochise Stronghold and would not get back until some time that evening. It was now about four in the afternoon. Taking a pair of field glasses, I climbed up into the cupola of the courthouse, sweeping the Cochise Stronghold with the glass, hoping to locate smoke from a campfire, which would disclose the position of the Wallace party, intending if smoke was found to send a rider to bring in Dr. Wallace. Returning to the hospital after my failure to locate Wallace from the top of the courthouse, I found Dr. Jones had, upon hearing about Burgano, gone down to check on things. I told Dr. Jones that Wallace could not be located and said I was going to wire Dr. Caven in Bisbee to come over. Jones said that would not be necessary, telling me he could perform the operation.

Enough said. Everything was ready, tools sterilized, so I called to Jones to get ready, walked into the surgical ward, picked up Burgano, and carrying him to the operating room, placed him on the table. I started giving him the chloroform, a job for which I was trained by Dr. Bacon.

In order that the reader can understand what followed, it is necessary to call attention to a previous case which called for a trepanning operation and which Dr. Bacon, in performing, had thoroughly explained to me. A patient had been brought into the hospital from Fairbanks where he had been found in a boxcar, shot in the right temple, the bullet ranging from the temple straight through to the back of the head. This man could not see or talk; he was placed on a bed in a separate room while arrangements were made to take care of him. As the gun had evidently been exploded close to the skull, the bone was badly fractured at the point of entry. This called for the use of the trepan saw which is a circular saw with a center punch set; that is, there is a sharp nail-like center in order to hold the saw in place.

Bacon always explained his operations to me; explained the setting of the center of the saw, the prying up of the fractured fragments, and especially cautioned me to be careful about too much pressure on the saw when trepanning in the neighborhood of the temple. He exphasized the large artery just under the bone, which, if punctured, would cause one to lose the patient.

Dr. Jones had thoroughly sterilized himself and was ready, Burgano had gone through the excitement stage and had reached a relaxed condition when I nodded to Jones to commence. First it was necessary to bare enough surface of the skull before the trepan saw could be used. Metal claws are always used to keep the skin from interfering but Jones kept using his fingers to hold the flap out of his way. This provoked me and grabbing up a set of the claws I hooked them in on two sides of the wound asking Jones if he had never used them. It was here that I commenced to doubt the ability of Jones to do the operation. Enough space had been bared on the skull to allow the use of the saw. I handed the saw to Jones but he seemed unable to get the center set right, causing considerable delay. I grabbed the saw, adjusted the center set and handed it back to him. Jones, putting all his weight on the saw, commenced to cut out the circular piece of bone through which leverage could be used to pry up the fractured pieces of skull and put them back into place. When I saw that Jones was going to ride the saw right on through, I grabbed it away from him and finished the operation myself. Had Jones continued with the pressure he was putting on the saw, when he finally broke clear through the skull, he would probably have cut the temple artery and the patient would have been lost. Jones accepted my taking over, evidently realizing that he was in over his head; he took my place giving the chloroform and the operation continued. The fractured bones were pried into place and small pieces of bone picked out of the wound. Jones at this point wanted to sew up the wound; I, however, refused, placing in the wound a short piece of rubber hose in which I clipped out a number of openings to allow for drainage, strapped the skin flaps back in place by the use of adhesive tape and the operation was over.

Wallace got back from the picnic about midnight and rushed to the hospital at once, believing he had an immediate operation to perform. I took him to the surgical ward, Wallace removed the bandage, stared in surprise and turning to me asked who had done it. I explained; Jones said that he also had witnessed a trepanning operation years ago and gave me the credit for the success of the operation. The job lacked the silver plate which is usually placed over the opening to protect the brain area, for no plate was available. But as long as

Burgano would live, it would be easy to see the beating of his pulse in the place on his right temple where the opening had been made.

I will always be thankful that the operation succeeded, and that I had the ability to protect my employer from a lawsuit. Both Dr. Bacon and Dr. Wallace insisted that I should go to school and become a surgeon. As this called for four years schooling, I was unable to find the time or the money to do so.

Owing to the wonderful climate of Tombstone and vicinity, Cochise County was a mecca for many people suffering from tuberculosis. The hospital was overflowing with these poor patients, and because it was hard to control the sanitary conditions I commenced to have a fear of contracting the disease myself. So I gave Dr. Bacon thirty days' notice that I was going to quit. He tried to talk me out of it, but I insisted.

Billy Tomlinson of the Silver Thread

Having left the employ of Doctor Bacon for whom I had been working for almost two years as steward of the Cochise County Hospital, I was looking for a job. Old man Grow was operating the Silver Thread Mine on the flat just below the old Contention shaft; in fact, the Thread had been running for years under the supervision of Billy Tomlinson. C. L. Cummings, who had been one of my pardners when mining in the Swisshelms and who had recommended me to Bacon in the first place, was in agreement with me that the danger of contracting tuberculosis was too great for me to continue working at the hospital. As he knew Mr. Grow, he introduced me to him, telling him he had a young man who was looking for a job. Grow looked me over, then told me his foreman, Tomlinson, did all the hiring and firing at the Silver Thread and I would have to take my chances with him.

At seven the next morning I was at the Silver Thread and tackled Tomlinson for a job. He had no opening so he asked me to come up every morning at seven—"Some morning I may have a place for you." Tomlinson did his own tool sharpening and tempering and after seeing his crew on the mine cage ready for work he almost always went to the blacksmith shop and sharpened up the dull drill steel on hand. I would also spend a little time in the shop and sometimes would face up a drill when Tomlinson was called out for a moment. I had been working at the hospital for almost two years, had done no hard work of any kind, so my muscles were rather soft and flabby. Well, one morning I found Tomlinson cutting up some new steel into lengths from six to eighteen inches. Drill steel is seven-eighths of an inch in diameter and is made from the toughest of good steel. The cutting of the different lengths called for a helper to use an eight-pound sledge to do the striking with. I grabbed up the hammer and helped Tomlinson cut up the steel into different lengths and to flatten the ends a little to aid when the real facing job commences. There were about eighteen pieces to be shaped up; this is precision work, for the different lengths have to be graduated down, the starter six-inch drills have the wider bit. Tomlinson placed about four pieces of steel in the forge with me helping him on the bellows. He knew I had sharpened my own steel in the Swisshelms, so did not hesitate to ask me to try my hand when he was suddenly called out of the shop by one of the men.

Tomlinson left and I started on the eighteen pieces of

Jams and Jamborees

In latter days I've heard lots of complaining about hard work and the harder job of finding anybody who really wants to do it. In the Old West I think it was different. Work was all over the place and everybody had to do it and there didn't seem to be much trouble about it. It wasn't work as much as play that got people in hot water. Come a holiday and a man might find himself with a problem on his hands. Like July Fourth, when we were near Casa Grande. It was about June 20 when it dawned on me that if something was not done to keep the key men on the job and they went into Tucson for Independence Day, we might be too crippled to operate for several days after the Fourth.

So I asked the town of Casa Grande to put on some sort of program in honor of the day. Had Hodges, our bookkeeper, sent a written challenge to Roman Cruz who operated the only store in Casa Grande and was manager of the Santa Cruz Reservoir and Land Co. baseball team, the local ball club.

The request was for a game of ball to be played July 4, and the challenge was accepted. Now the problem was to get a team together.

I had Major Wright, head of our surveyors, lay out a diamond, using gunny sacks filled with sand for bases.

Everyone got interested and tried out for positions. We quickly found that we had only three players who had ever played ball, so we tried out everyone for his batting ability.

I'll never forget when Charlie Monroe got up to see what he could do. Someone hollered "Give him a manure shovel!" Charlie was our barn man and took care of our stock. We quickly found, however, that Charlie was some batter. He could hit anything!

Stafford, another one of the surveyors, had pitched a little in college. A young man—I have forgotten his name—had played first base, while Charlie White, brother of Scott White, had at some time learned how to catch.

So, we had only three men who had ever played baseball in their lives—a pitcher, a catcher, and a first baseman.

The Fourth of July arrived—a hot, bright summer day, and we got ready to head for the dusty desert town of Casa Grande. The game was to start at 2 p.m. About noon I got the entire team in and on the running boards of the Reo car which the Company furnished and we started for Casa Grande to meet the opposing team.

We immediately drove out to the ballfield, and starting at home base I drove the car, circling around first, second, and third and back to home plate, saying as we drove around the bases, "I'm doing this to show you fellows the way around for we have a tough game to play and win."

Before the game we outlined our strategy. The first man to get on first base was to go down to second on the first ball pitched. Under no circumstances were we to deviate from this plan. As a result, the pitcher, the catcher, and the second baseman on the opposing team were quickly under pressure. The upshot was we won a game we had no business winning, and the final score was 31 to 19 in our favor.

Casa Grande put on a July Fourth dance that night, but thanks to the ordeal of the day, I was so stiff and sore I couldn't even go to the dance, much less dance when I got there. I went to bed instead, and it took me a full week to get over that ball game.

But we made our point. When the fifth of July arrived we were back on the job and able to operate without losing any of our main crew.

* * *

Another time there was a big celebration in Tombstone when the railroad finally reached the town and rails were laid into the city limits—along about April 12, 1903. All the townspeople were out to watch the track-ending ceremonies, and with the noise and excitement a team of mules took fright. They bolted and threatened fair to run at top speed right into the crowds of women and children.

I saw the team running wild, heading for the intersection of Fourth and Allen where the crowds were, so I ran up the street, turned and started running with the team. I grabbed the off mule by its bridle, while running alongside, reached across and got hold of the other mule's bridle, and yanking back was able to bring the crazy critters to a halt, within just a few feet of the rows of women and children seated on boxes at the street intersection.

The Tombstone *Epitaph* and the *Daily Prospector* both printed items about this "holiday event." The *Epitaph* for Monday evening, April 13, tells the story thus:

The hero of the day yesterday was Fireman Max Axford, who showed the metal he was made of by stopping a runaway dray team that was dashing into the thickest of the crowd on Allen street before the horse race. The runaways were headed for the Can Can porch when brave Max caught them by the bridle reins just in time to prevent them from trampling the crowd of women and children gathered there.

The *Daily Prospector* wrote as follows:

One of the bravest acts ever performed in Tombstone was done yesterday by Max Axford when he stopped the runaway team of mules by heroically hanging on to the bridle and stopping them just this side of a large crowd of ladies and children on the corner of Fourth and Allen.

Here was a case where knowledge was mistaken for bravery. There was no extraordinary "dedication" on my part whatsoever. Just before coming to Tombstone I had been earning my beans by breaking a large number of wild horses to saddle and ride. Handling a runaway team was all in the day's work for me.

Nevertheless the crowd hoisted me up on their shoulders, carried me to a saloon close by, set me up on the bar, and the town was mine.

* * *

I have heard from the old timers too, that even in the earliest days danger most likely reared its head when the workday was over and it was time to play. During the years I lived in Tombstone, I became acquainted with many of its citizens, good and bad—and there were both kinds, just as in any other town. I knew W. Stahley, the district attorney; Allen R. English, Tombstone's celebrated criminal lawyer; Martin Costello, the saloon keeper; sheriffs Scott White, Del Lewis, and Stewart Hunt, and listened to many stories about the early day characters—tales fresh from citizens who lived in Tombstone when these things happened.

I got this tale from Uncle Joe Tasker. Buckskin Frank Leslie in early Tombstone days was considered not only the fastest man on the draw but also a dead shot. The Earps, Doc Holliday—in fact all the most celebrated characters you have heard of, were careful not to offend Leslie.

Russian Bill, among others, had a meeting with Leslie, according to Uncle Joe. There was bad feeling between Russian Bill and Buckskin Frank Leslie over one of Tombstone's redlight favorites. Russian Bill was a member of Curly Bill's gang of cattle rustlers who were engaged in stealing Mexican cattle in Mexico and crossing them into Arizona territory where they were usually sold to the United States Army forces. After a good haul of this kind, then came the celebration. Curly Bill's gang usually spent several days drinking and gambling amid the comforts and charms of good old Tombstone.

Leslie had a ranch located on the eastern side of the Swisshelm Mountains in a valley lying between these mountains and the south end of the Chiricahuas. In addition to his bartending, Leslie was trying to build up a small cattle spread. His brand was 7-UP connected.

Uncle Joe Tasker had a little saloon and stopping place at what was known as the Soldier Holes where soldiers used to camp when chasing Apaches in the early days. Soldier Holes was situated in the middle of the great Sulphur Springs Valley at a point about halfway between Tombstone and Buckskin's ranch in the Swiss-helms and about eight miles north of the Mexican border. In making the trip on horseback between Tombstone and his ranch, Buckskin usually reached Uncle Joe's place about noon and had a couple of drinks and a good meal before continuing his ride to the ranch. Curly Bill and his gang, which included Russian Bill, often dropped in for a visit with Uncle Joe.

One day Buckskin was riding on one of his trips from Tombstone to his ranch, riding a little bay mare which started to go lame shortly after leaving Tombstone, and by the time Buckskin reached Uncle Joe's place the mare could hardly go on. It was necessary for Uncle Joe to put up Leslie and his mare for the night. Buckskin and Uncle Joe spent most of the afternoon in the bar room. Buck-skin, during this time, taught Uncle Joe the mysteries of several mixed drinks which of course had to be tried out after the mixing. It was getting along toward the middle of the afternoon, and already the shadows of the Mule Mountains to the west were halfway across Sulphur Springs Valley. About 4 o'clock, Buckskin and Uncle Joe heard a bunch of riders coming fast from the direction of Mexico. It was a part of Curly Bill's gang with Russian Bill in the lead. They pulled up in a cloud of dust and as Russian Bill dismounted he yelled, "I'm Russian Bill, a wolf with a red eye and it's my day to howl!"

Bill was the first to enter, the rest of the gang framed the doorway behind him when Russian Bill was stopped dead in his tracks by Buckskin's voice asking, "Bill, how much money have you got on you?" Bill looked at Leslie and realized that this was a showdown which called for an answer or else. Bill's answer came slow. "About eighty, Frank."

"Put it up on the bar," said Leslie. Bill walked over and threw the money on the bar. Leslie, waving his hand to Bill's gang in the doorway behind him said, "Drink it up boys—it's Bill's day to howl." This was a tough challenge in front of Russian Bill's friends and no doubt hard to take. Russian Bill was later hung in Galeyville for, of all things, stealing a horse. Buckskin Leslie spent several years in the pen at Yuma for being too fast with the use of his 45.

* * *

But even the soberest kind of social gathering could be the occasion for a heated exchange of words, or sometimes it might be just a joke, but the old timers were pretty sensitive, and the right joke in the wrong place usually didn't make a hit.

Colonel William Herring of Tucson was an attorney for the railroad interests in the early days.

The Colonel was a very large man. He stood over six feet tall, had an enormous bay window, and weighed about 260 or 275 pounds. No doubt he was somewhat self-conscious about his large size. He was also a loyal attendant at the Chamber of Commerce weekly luncheons, very dignified social occasions attended only by the most solid of citizens.

The chairman presiding at one of those luncheon meetings evidently had a big growth too—an oversized bump of humor. Soon as the Colonel was seated, he addressed him, saying, "I see, Colonel, you are getting to be quite a favorite of the railroad."

"How's that?" asked the Colonel.

"Why, I see where they have named a station up on the Mohave Desert in your honor."

"Is that so, I have not heard. What did they call it?"

"Mammoth Tank," said the chairman.

The story goes that the Colonel pushed his chair back, reached for his hat, walked out of the room, and never attended another Chamber of Commerce luncheon.

* * *

As time went on, tempers seemed to cool down a little bit—even around Tombstone. Things got so you could have a big time one night and go back to work the next day, and even July Fourth didn't threaten a three-day stoppage of all work.

Russian Bill, Frank Leslie, and other well-known characters of the Old West became legendary figures in Arizona history. Perhaps it's because so much of that history managed to stay alive in the heads of a few old-timers that the officials for Tombstone's annual Helldorado selected me—a campfire story-teller—for parade marshal in 1968. The three-day October celebration—historical pageant, fair, and general jamboree—has served as a sort of memory book come to life, so that modern young Westerners can see with their own eyes some of what went on in the tales told around Western Campfires, the jams as well as the jamborees.

Some Early Day Trials

Many early day Tombstone citizens were entertained by the colorful trials of Allen R. English, Tombstone's most celebrated lawyer. One we will call Frenchy's lament. The Boquillas Land and Cattle Company had won the long fight to get title to the old Spanish land grant which covered most of its holdings. For years this title had been in dispute and during those years many settlers had moved in on the land as squatters and could not be legally removed from the homes which they had established. They built houses and sheds, fenced in pastures for their stock and made the many improvements so necessary for a livable home.

With the court decision granting title to the company was a court order to reimburse all the settlers for the improvements made on these lands. An appraisal committee was formed and in due time turned in the amounts agreed upon by the committee. Several squatters would not accept the amounts offered and suits were started in the courts to reimburse them for what they considered the improvements to be worth.

One of the squatters was a Frenchman whom everyone called Frenchy. Among Frenchy's improvements was a pond about fifty feet in diameter which was kept filled by a windmill close by. Frenchy wanted eight hundred dollars for the pond which had been listed by the appraisers at one hundred and fifty dollars. The famous early day lawyer Allan English represented the company and went after Frenchy under cross-examination. It went as follows:

"Frenchy, how many days did it take you to make this pond?"

"Two-and-a-half days."

"How did you build it?"

"With two teams and Fresno scrapers."

"How much did you have to pay for the teams?"

"Five dollars a day for team and driver."

"At five dollars a day for two-and-a-half days for two teams, that's a total of twenty-five dollars. How do you ask eight hundred dollars for a pond which you admit cost you only twenty-five dollars to build?"

"Good God! English, I have eight hundred dollars worth of frogs in that pond."

This brought a roar of laughter from the court room as few people in those days considered frogs to be edible. However to Frenchy this was serious for he loved frog legs and had succeeded lately in selling several dozen to the Can Can Restaurant.

Frenchy was compelled, however, to accept the one hundred and fifty dollars offered in settlement. And Tombstone for years laughed about Frenchy's eight-hundred-dollar frog pond.

Another case called for some master handling by English in order to arrive at an answer to the question, "When is a man legally drunk?" This was a tough case involving some cattle rustling where a calf had been branded and showed up following a cow with another brand. The calf plainly showed rope marks where it had been tied up. There was no doubt that the prisoner was guilty but to get a jury that would bring in a guilty verdict was some problem.

Allan English was at his best after he had taken on three or four stiff jolts of whiskey and every morning on his way down to the court house made about three stops on his walk down the street. On his first stop at the Crystal Palace one morning, English came in just in time to see a notorious cowman, who was on the jury panel, hoisting a morning drink. Allan was anxious to get this fellow off the panel for he well knew if he stayed on it would surely mean a hung jury.

Court convened and Allan was examining the prospective jurymen when the name of the cowman whom he was anxious to get rid of came up. English went after him hard; he had used most of his exemptions and wanted an excuse to oust this fellow without losing any of his rights. In the middle of the examination he suddenly asked the prospective juryman, "How many drinks does it take to make you drunk?"

"About ten," was the answer.

"How many drinks have you had this morning?"

The man knew that English had seen him take one

drink. "I have taken one drink," was the answer. English turned to the judge–"Your Honor, I challenge the jury on the grounds that this man is one-tenth drunk."

I do not know the outcome as I was called out of the court room at this moment, but I have always wondered just what decision the judge made.

Stahley was another prominent lawyer and also a noted wit and Tombstone still chuckles over some of Stahley's sayings. He was district attorney for Cochise county, Arizona, and in this capacity it was his duty to pass upon the different expense accounts turned in by the county officials. Biddy Doyle was constable at Bisbee, and Stahley had objected to several items of expense turned in by Doyle, amounting to about two hundred dollars. Doyle had made the trip to Tombstone to try to talk Stahley into allowing the items in dispute. But Stahley stood pat, and Doyle, losing his head, had tried to attack Stahley in his office but was held off by friends of both. The next morning, after Doyle's attempted attack, they met in front of the Can Can Restaurant on their way to breakfast. Doyle shook his fist at Stahley as they went in, saying, "Stahley, if you do not allow my claim, I am going to work you over."

Due to the large crowd in the restaurant, only two seats were available and Stahley and Doyle were seated at the same table. The waiter came to the table and with pencil poised asked, "What will it be, gentlemen?"

"Boxing gloves for two," answered Stahley. This broke the ice–even Doyle had to smile, and said afterwards, "How in the world could one stay mad with a man like Stahley?"

Stahley and English were both lawyers and both heavy drinkers and found themselves running against each other for district attorney. For years they had been alternating the office, one term for Stahley, the next for English. But this time they were pitted against each other and Cochise County settled back to enjoy the fireworks. Stahley always had a quick comeback—English was more subtle, a master of the English language, but it sometimes took a moment or two before the average person could get his meaning.

They were traveling together and holding meetings all over Cochise County. When approaching a little settlement where they were both to talk that night, they were stopped by a flood of water in a wash that usually was dry. There had been heavy rains along the slope of the mountains and both the Stahley and the English parties were forced to stay all night with a rancher waiting for the water to recede. In the morning the wash was dry and the parties continued on their way. Stahley had been getting the best of English in the verbal exchanges between them, but that night English had Stahley, for a moment, stopped in his tracks. English apologized for failure to keep their schedule, explaining that high water on an unusually dry wash had held them up. He then proceeded to eulogize on Stahley, telling what a wonderful man he was and how lucky Cochise County was to have such an illustrious citizen; further said he felt something suitable should be done for him like naming a mountain or some landmark in his honor. So I hereby make a motion that the dry wash which held us up last night be hereafter known as Stahley Creek, 'Always full at night and dry the next morning.'

For once Stahley was bowled over and could not think of a suitable comeback. It was not until the last day of the campaign that a suitable reply presented itself. When crossing the San Pedro River at Fairbanks on the way in, Stahley found the answer. So that night at the final grand rally Stahley made his comeback. He called attention to the praise that English had given him, how he had named a dry wash "Stahley Creek" in his honor, because it was always full at night and dry the next morning. He went on to say that he had been stumped for a suitable reply until they were on their way home when they crossed the San Pedro River. "Ladies and gentlemen, I now make a motion that the name of the San Pedro River be changed to English River, because it is full *all* the time."

I here recall a story of two officers which would indicate it makes a difference which side of the law you are on. Porter McDonald and Billy Stiles were at one time both officers of the law. Porter remained true to his chosen occupation, but Stiles turned to train robbery and betrayed the profession. When Stiles was an officer he, at one time, had occasion to arrest Porter for a minor infraction of the town's laws. He walked with Porter down to the City Hall to get things straightened out and made no effort to use handcuffs.

Years later Stiles and Mat Bunts held up the first section of a Southern Pacific passenger, mail and express train at Cochise Station, a few miles west of Willcox, Arizona. Burt Alvord, an inside pardner of Stiles, had been arrested and was confined in the jail at Tombstone. Stiles held up George Bravin, the jailer; in the melee shot Bravin through the leg, and liberated Alvord. Several weeks later a Mexican by the name of Taos notified the sheriff's office that Stiles was to visit his wife who at the time was living in a tent a few miles above Hereford on the San Pedro River. The Sheriff's office sent Porter McDonald who was then head deputy down to look into the report.

A number of ranchers had joined the Mexican, Taos,

and were ready to join Porter in making the arrest. Porter was late in getting to Hereford and it was quite dark when he arrived. About midnight the posse surrounded the tent and Porter went inside. Striking a match over the man and woman in the bed, he found a man with a heavy growth of beard and not recognizing Stiles, went outside and told the posse that there was a man in there all right, but he did not think it was Stiles. Taos assured Porter that it was Stiles. Porter went back into the tent, lit a lamp on the table and punching Stiles in the ribs told him, "Get up, Billy, you're under arrest." Porter immediately handcuffed Stiles and they started for Tombstone. Stiles told Porter that as a fellow officer he was humiliating him by using handcuffs on him and reminded him of the time that Stiles had arrested Porter, saying, "I did not handcuff you." "No," Porter said, "you were not afraid of me but you are a desperado now, and I am taking no chances. I am afraid of you now that I have you arrested." Porter had no fear of Stiles when he was looking him over with a lighted match, but with Stiles under arrest it was different and until he was safe in the Tombstone jail, Porter was riding scared.

The Sale of the Irish Mag

Martin Costello was the owner of a saloon in Tombstone; this story will tell you how and why Daley turned over the Irish Mag mining claims to Costello and how Costello afterwards sold the Irish Mag for $550,000.

Daley lived near what later became Lowell, just south of Bisbee, on the highway to Douglas, and was the owner of a number of mining claims known as the Irish Mag, which claims butted up against the Copper Queen claims to the north. Daley was a periodical drinker and about every two or three weeks would go on a bender and shoot up the little settlement. When this happened someone would ride up to Bisbee and make a complaint, and as

Bisbee was the only town with a deputy sheriff, the deputy would ride down and arrest Daley and put him in the Bisbee jail. This happened so many times that Daley began to suspect that the Copper Queen Company was having him thrown into jail because they wanted his Irish Mag claims. Thoroughly convinced that this was true, when let out of jail the last time, he told the deputy sheriff, "The next time you come after me, come a-shooting." Things rolled along on an even keel for several weeks, then Daley went on one of his famous drunks and riding up and down the canyon, threatened everyone and especially those he termed the Copper Queen hirelings. Daley was reported, as usual, and the Deputy rode down again to arrest him, but this time Daley made good his threat and shot and killed the deputy. Daley notified his wife—he was married to a Mexican woman—got on his horse and rode out of the country.

Martin Costello, a Tombstone saloon-keeper, used to hunt often on the flat country east of Tombstone, using a two-wheeled cart to which he harnessed a white mare. Daley, in leaving, was cutting across the country and seeing Martin with his old white mare, rode over and notified him that he had killed the deputy and was compelled to leave the country. He told Costello to do the assessment work on the Irish Mag Claims, and he would keep him advised of his whereabouts. Costello gave Daley what money he had with him and Daley rode on. Costello kept the assessment work done on the Irish Mag for several years.

Time marched on. The Calumet and Hecla Company in upper Michigan, looking for new copper prospects, noting that the Irish Mag joined the Copper Queen on the south, sent one of its men to Bisbee to get a job in the Queen and check out the lay of the ore bodies. The supposition is that with the use of a compass he found that the large sulphide bodies pitched under the Irish Mag at about one thousand feet depth. They contacted Costello in Tombstone and made an offer of $550,000 for the Irish Mag property. Costello, who was in touch with Daley, got a signed bill of sale from him, but as Daley was married it was also necessary to get his Mexican wife to sign the papers before the sale could be completed. Old Man Reilly was Costello's attorney; they contacted Mrs. Daley, offered her a certified check for $25,000 to sign the papers, but she refused to sign. Costello was furious but Mrs. Daley could not be stampeded into signing anything and the more they insisted the more stubborn she became. It was a sad situation—here was $550,000 waiting to be paid as soon as Mrs. Daley's signature was obtained. Costello in desperation told Old Man Reilly he would give almost any sum to get her to sign.

Lawyer Reilly was also married to a Mexican woman, so at lunch one day he told his wife about the trouble they were having trying to get Mrs. Daley to sign. Mrs. Reilly understanding her people, asked Reilly how they offered the money to Mrs. Daley. "Why, we offered her a $25,000 certified check," and showed her the check. "No wonder she did not sign—she was afraid of the check. Reilly, I'll tell you what to do; get $5,000 in one dollar bills, walk in and throw the money on her kitchen table and offer her all of it to sign." Costello and Reilly followed her advice, heaped the $5,000 in one dollar bills on the table, offering it all if she would sign. Mrs. Daley could understand this pile of bills, five thousand of them, but she could not understand a check worth $25,000, and the Irish Mag claims were transferred to the Calumet and Arizona Mining Company, making several millions for the owner during its lifetime.

There is some kind of moral involved here; the only one I can think of at the moment is: A deal is a good one if it makes both sides happy. Mrs. Daley was happy with her five thousand one dollar bills and Costello was doubly happy with the Reilly deal. Costello I believe, died in Tucson several years later.

When the Pearce Mine in Sulphur Springs Valley was discovered, it led to an answer from Mrs. Johnny Pearce that has brought many a smile to the residents in the locality. In the middle of Sulphur Springs Valley in Cochise County is a small cluster of hills. On one of these hills lay a long snake-like ledge of white quartz. White quartz, as any mining man will tell you, is often a carrier of gold. In fact, most of the gold ledges in the mother lode country of California are composed more or less of this white quartz.

Tombstone, about thirty miles to the west, had been established in 1877 by a prospector named Ed Schieffelin and for many years numerous men had passed by this white quartz ledge without its value being discovered. Among them were Curly Bill, John Ringo, Buckskin Frank Leslie, Russian Bill and the other noted early-day bad men; also noted sheriffs, such as Johnny Behan, John Slaughter and Breckenridge, and employes of the Chiricahua Cattle Company and the Erie Cattle Company, which outfits grazed their herds around this little cluster of hills.

No doubt many samples assayed from the ledge by Abbott, the commercial assayer in Tombstone, had showed only a trace of the yellow metal. As stated, many men had often passed by this ledge but ignored it with the thought that if anything of value was there it would have been discovered years ago. This did not mean however that the ledge was barren, for it was one of nature's freaks.

In 1894, seventeen years after the settling of Tombstone, a cow puncher passing by whose name was Herman Durand (if my memory is correct) broke off a sample of the quartz which for some unknown reason looked promising to him. While on his way to Tombstone he went a little out of his way in order to go by the Johnny Pearce Ranch which was in the foothills of the Dragoon Mountains to the west. Giving Pearce the samples he had taken from the ledge he told him they looked promising to him and advised Pearce to go up and take a look, remarking that he would be able to see where these samples had been broken from the ledge.

A couple of days later Pearce, in riding by, changed his course and on a hunch rode up on the hill, found where Durand had taken his samples, broke off a few more pieces and sent them in to Abbott to assay. When the report came back, showing several hundred dollars in gold per ton, Johnny Pearce would not believe it. Pearce however had kept what is known as an umpire assay, that is, he had kept one-half of the original sample sent in to Abbott. He sent this half to the Colorado Fuel and Iron Smelters in Pueblo, Colorado, to be checked. The umpire assay confirmed Abbott's report.

In the meantime he had located his claim, taking in the entire length of the white ledge. Pearce, who was a Cousin Jack miner, started work on the claim, sinking a shaft at the point where the samples had been taken. For about ten or twelve feet at this point on the ledge was the only spot of value on the entire ledge; a chimney of ore had shot through to the surface at this point. This accounts for the many years which passed before this one spot had been sampled. All other assays from the ledge had proven barren.

In no time at all Pearce had a carload of ore on its way to the smelter in El Paso. When the work reached a depth of sixty or seventy feet the ore chimney had widened out until he had a chute of ore about thirty feet in width and seventy feet in depth. Again, Pearce soon had two or three cars of ore in transit to the smelter. The ore was hauled in wagons to Cochise Station on the Southern Pacific and shipped from there to the smelter.

As news of a strike travels fast, in a few weeks time a party showed up and offered Pearce $250,000 for a working monthly lease, all ore to be left on the mine's dump until the sale was completed. Pearce told the man that he would have to take it up with Mrs. Pearce, so they rode over to the ranch to discuss it with her. They called to Mrs. Pearce to come out and join them, having stopped their horses at the yard fence. When she joined them, Mr. Pearce told her that they had an offer of $250,000 for the mine and asked if she was agreeable to sell for this price. She evidently had no sense of the value of money for after thinking it over for a moment answered in what has become one of the classic answers of the West. "We will accept this offer provided you will give me the right to run the boarding house at the mine." The buyer refused, saying he intended to reserve that right for his own wife.

Anyway the mine was sold and for many years, the Pearce Mine was a rich producer, yielding about $15,000,000 before running out of ore. What Herman Durand got out of this has never been mentioned. The most disgusted man in Arizona however was a rancher, Sam Coleman; it seems Sam had at one time broken off a sample of this chimney of ore three years before and had left the piece lying on his porch all this time, intending some day to have it assayed. After the discovery, Sam, by using a powerful mineral glass, could easily see specks of free gold in his sample.

I Hire Out to Big Del Lewis

Big Del Lewis, sheriff of Cochise County, was worried. Another jail break had taken place and nineteen prisoners had escaped; last year the same thing had happened, causing the sheriff to spend several thousand dollars before the escaped prisoners were recaptured and Big Del did not relish a repeat of the hours of hard riding with its attendant hardships and expense which this break apparently was also going to cause.

For years it had been the custom to give older men the job of supervising and guarding the Tombstone jail and Farrington, his present jailer, was one of these, past middle-age and weighing around two hundred thirty pounds. Del had talked things over with Porter Mc-Donald, his head deputy, and Callahan, his office man, and they had all agreed that the next jailer should be a younger man. While going over a list of younger prospects, none of whom seemed to fill the bill, Porter suggested that they hire me. I had worked with Porter on the 7-D Ranch where I broke horses one winter for the 7-D's. I had never met Big Del, although I knew him by sight, and was I surprised one day while crossing the street to have him stop me and ask what I was doing. I told him nothing at the moment and he asked me if I could handle the jail job and guarantee that no prisoners would escape. I told him I was sure I could handle the job, but before making a guarantee, I would like to have a look at the premises and the guard personnel. Del pulled out a notebook from his jacket pocket, wrote an order to jailer Farrington to let me in to look over the setup, saying as he handed me the note that he would be waiting for me in his office when I came out.

I presented the note to Farrington, was admitted and went over the personnel list, conditions to be met and the like. I then asked Farrington to let me inside with the prisoners, as I wanted to see the position of windows, the method of locking cell doors; in fact, everything that would help me make the guarantee which the sheriff demanded. I found that there were six guards including the jailer Farrington; that two men were on each shift of eight hours; that the guards spent most of their time sitting out in front playing cards or checkers and went inside among the prisoners only when something needed attention. In talking with Farrington and Briggs, the guard then on duty, I found that the tools which were used to dig a hole through the brick wall in the last break were brought into the jail by trusties who had been employed by Mrs. Lewis in yard and stable work.

After going over everything thoroughly I felt I could make Del his guarantee, provided that I would be the boss and not subject to any interference from anybody. On my way out I stopped in at the office and found Big Del, Porter, and Callahan waiting for me. Del asked me what was my decision. I told him I would guarantee no one would escape provided I was the boss, no trusty was to go out any place unless accompanied by a guard and I was to hire and fire the guards; if I found a guard was not dependable I wanted the right to remove him without political interference.

I shall always believe that because of the two jail breaks with the added expense attached, Big Del was willing to agree to almost anything in order to get someone to take the job who would make a guarantee. Anyway, I took on Farrington's job, immediately separated the guards, putting one inside to mix with the prisoners and keep his eyes and ears open at all times. The inside guard was to be unarmed at all times—under no circumstances was an armed man to be allowed inside.

The jail in Tombstone at that time had eighty-five prisoners for crimes all the way from petty larceny to murder and everything in between. I found that outside of a couple of decks of cards the prisoners had no way of amusing themselves, so I bought a set of boxing gloves, checker boards and a couple of harmonicas in order to have a little music once in a while. The Mexicans soon added to our music by having friends loan them a guitar and a violin and before long we had good music on tap.

Among the prisoners was a barber; alongside the west of the courthouse and adjoining the jail quarters was an exercise yard surrounded by an eighteen or twenty foot brick wall. Here I set the barber up, giving him a few extra privileges provided his hair-cutting and shaving services could be used by the prisoners. This barber setup perked up the prisoners and soon they spent some of their time improving their personal appearance. The more active one could keep the prisoners the less time they would have to think of means to break out. With cards, boxing gloves, and music we had a very active group of men.

A new addition to the jail had been made which included about forty cells enclosed in a square cell block with two long corridors; the cells were closed and locked by a lever system on each side of the front corridor doors. By pulling a lever, all doors could be locked or opened. This cell structure was one-and-three-quarter inches wide by three-eighths inch thick flat steel bars which were supposed to be made of chilled steel which no steel saw could cut through. I soon found out that the steel workers who built the cell addition hid three hacksaws somewhere inside and advised the prisoners of their whereabouts. Understanding that the new cell block was constructed of chilled steel I was not much worried about it. I figured what I would have to watch was the round, three-quarter inch iron bars which protected the long double windows, of which there were about seven, counting the one in the toilet.

On my shift, the morning shift from seven to three, I usually spent at least half of the time on the inside and Briggs taking half likewise. Whenever I gave my word on anything to a person I never backed down on it; this soon built up a reputation with the men that my word could be depended upon. This was to help me later when things got rougher.

About this time Big Del brought in a prisoner by the name of Kennibrew and told me when we were checking him in that he was the toughest customer he had ever encountered, that I should put him in one of the cell blocks and keep him there. Kennibrew's face was one large scab; he had busted a window out of the toilet on the train and propelled himself head first off the train which was traveling about thirty-five or forty miles per hour at the time. He was lucky to be alive. After Del left I sat down and talked to Kennibrew, called his attention to what the sheriff had advised but told him instead I was going to give him a break—I would not put him in a block cell but would treat him the same as the other prisoners and as long as he conducted himself properly he would be well treated. The crime with which Kennibrew was charged was attempted murder.

Things rolled along on an even keel until one day in making a quick inspection of the men's rest room, I found one of the hacksaw blades lying on the floor and when I picked it up the blade was still warm, showing it had just been in use. I immediately examined the round bars in the window and found that one of them had been sawed about a third of the way through. By getting possession of this one saw I still had two to go. Kennibrew so far had been giving no trouble—one could not have asked for a more model prisoner. I had adopted the policy of never asking a prisoner for information; I quickly found that prisoners will come to you but if you ask them to tell you something they will immediately clam up. I was soon informed that Kennibrew knew where the last two saws were hidden and was organizing a group and that an attempt to break out was to be made. Instead of putting Kennibrew in solitary at this time, I left things just as they were, for I wanted an attempt to saw out to be made; I felt safe with the chilled steel bars on the cell block, but to protect myself with the outside windows I put an extra guard outside with a shotgun to guard the windows.

It was getting close to circuit court time and several of the prisoners, knowing their own guilt, were getting rather nervous as the time for their trials approached. As the grand jury and circuit court met only twice a year, a prisoner sometimes remained in the county jail for three to five months before his case would come before the grand jury and if indicted he quickly went to trial in the circuit court.

I had built up a reputation for squareness with the prisoners, resulting in information being constantly given me about how things were going. This information was passed to me in different ways, sometimes by just a word or two when passing by. I always kept my eyes open for any activity out of the ordinary; I made a round of the outside of the cell blocks about every fifteen minutes when I was on inside duty. On one of my rounds I saw a prisoner writing on a small piece of paper when I passed by; I continued on around and repeated the round; when I passed this prisoner's cell he wadded up the paper and tossed it out on the floor in front of me. I stooped to pick it up, walked to the front and asked Briggs to let me outside. I went into the front jail office out of sight of the jail, opened up the paper and found this message. "You will find one of the saws under the bottom iron on the left side of my cell—a wire will be found on the bunk to pull it out with."

I immediately returned, Briggs let me inside and when I reached the prisoner's cell he was still on his bed; he had not thought that I would go into immediate action so had not left the cell. I found the wire and running it along on the floor under the bottom iron, found the saw. I grabbed the prisoner by the nape of the neck and the seat of his pants, rushed him up to the block cells, threw him inside and asked Briggs to throw the lever locking him in. This was necessary in order to protect the prisoner. I was immediately surrounded by a bunch of the prisoners wanting to know what had happened. I explained that in making my rounds of inspection I had noticed the saw blade sticking out from under the floor iron of his cell and as the blade was in his cell I of course knew he had been using the saw. While talking to this bunch of prisoners I had unconsciously tried to bend the blade and, lo and behold, it bent easily showing that the temper had been completely taken out of it. I knew at once that considerable sawing had been done somewhere. Bending the saw I said to the boys that the saw was no good and thought I would give it back to them. Kennibrew spoke up saying he would give fifty dollars for a new one just like it. "Yes" I said to myself, "I had better find the place where the saw was used and find it fast." I got a small round looking glass and started examining the bars; figuring that the end of the corridor would be the most logical place, I proceeded to check it thoroughly. By holding the glass in my hand and running it along the bars I could see under each bar without stooping down, which would have called attention to my procedure. I quickly found the sawing; they had filled the resulting crack with soap which made it harder to discover. In examining the sawing I found that had they been able to saw just one more bar they could have made it out of that side of the cell block. Now this was supposed to be the chilled steel—providing a new jail which could not be sawed. I quickly contacted the local blacksmith, Ray

Swain, explaining what was necessary for repairs and had him come down to replace the damage.

As Kennibrew was mixed up in this sawing and due to the fact three convictions had been rendered in the circuit court, one of them for murder, I quickly put leg shackles on the four men and locked them in the four block cells which were separated from the main part of the jail. Owing to the fact that the guard who was on the inside the night the sawing was done was evidently not the man for the job, I let him go and hired a young man named Springer in his place.

Just as I was going off shift Kennibrew called me over to his cell and said, "Old timer, we will take these leg shackles off for you." While I did not think it could be done, I told Kennibrew that I had heard it could be done but I did not think they had brains enough to do the job. He asked if I would promise not to put them back on if they could take them off. I gave Kennibrew my promise and left for home, firmly believing that if it could be done they would do it.

At nine o'clock that night they phoned the house and told me that all shackles were off except the ones on Chapo Eridio, a Mexican boy convicted of murder. About ten o'clock the boys on night shift advised me that all shackles were off. I now faced a problem. I had promised that if the boys took off the shackles I would not put any more on them. I lay awake for some time before I figured out a way. I had made my promise, but what was in the way of having Big Del shackle them again. Up in the cupola of the Court House I had seen five sets of leg irons which had been used to shackle the five prisoners who were all hung at one time several years before. These leg shackles were put on with rivets. The problem now was to get the information and the names to the sheriff. Here is what I figured out.

On my way down the next morning I alerted Ray Swain, the blacksmith whose shop was two blocks away, to be ready with rivets and means with which to do the job, and told Ray that we would call him. When I arrived at the jail the four pair of leg shackles were hanging on the bars at the front of the jail. The boys all gathered around and told me that young Springer on his first shift had really lived up to his name. When he was making his rounds on the inside shift, they would throw a pair of shackles on the cement floor behind him and he would jump almost out of his shoes. We had quite a laugh over this—the boys were elated over the fact that the shackles had been taken off. "You know, boys," I suggested, "we ought to write a note to Big Del telling him to send coupons to Arbuckle Coffee for new shackles—that these are no good." I will take the shackles and the note over to Big Del. A note was hurriedly written, the four boys signed it and as I went out the door I heard on of them say, "I bet Big Del's eyes will bug out when he reads that note."

Del Lewis lived just across the street in front of the Court House. I crossed the street with the shackles on my arm, rang the front door bell and presented the shackles and note to Big Del when he came to the door. "My God! Axford, they are not going to break out, are they?" asked Lewis. "Don't worry, Del, they are not getting out but I have a job for you to do. I have promised that if they could take off the shackles I would not put them back on but there is nothing to keep you, as sheriff, from doing the job. The boys have signed this note, so you have all their names; I will have Swain, the blacksmith, join you in a few minutes. I am going uptown and when I return I expect to find the riveted leg irons all in place."

Big Del immediately got busy and when I returned I found all four hobbling around with the new leg irons on to stay. They at once gathered around me and one started to protest, when Kennibrew spoke up. "Well Axford lived up to his agreement; the trouble is with us. We should have known there was nothing to keep someone else in Cochise County from doing the job." "Boys," I said, "the greatest mistake was writing that damn note and signing your names." They all agreed to this. I had a little more trouble with Kennibrew; finally he called me over and asked if he would promise not to give me any more trouble would I take the leg irons off. He gave me his word, I cut the leg irons off and he made good his promise. When his case went before the grand jury, they refused to indict him and he was released.

The system I installed of using one guard inside and one out is, I believe, still in use, and Cochise County has been free of jail breaks to this day. However it takes a lot of figuring to outsmart clever prisoners. I soon found out that many able men get into prison; such a man was Chicago Whitey. We received this prisoner bound over to await the action of the grand jury for the crime of boxcar robbery. While he had a lot of personality, he was what you would call a professional tramp. When we checked him in he had a total sum on him of one dollar and seventy-five cents. At that time, if I remember right, we had about ninety prisoners in the county jail—a fairly large "enrollment."

Whitey looked the prisoners over. As the grand jury had just met, Whitey had about five months to wait before the next session. One day he approached me and asked if I had any objection to his making a little money, stated that he had noticed that all Mexicans had "a sweet tooth" and he wanted to have a one-burner oil stove, a couple of small fry pans, some flour, sugar and dried fruit; said he wanted to make what he called Mexican pies and sell them to the other prisoners. As he had only one dollar and seventy-five cents he asked if I would help him out in getting started. Well, I bought him a secondhand one-burner stove, a couple of fry pans, donated flour, sugar, lard and dried fruit from my home, and he was on his way to his first million.

He stewed the dried apples and raisins, well sweetened and flavored with cinnamon, and made a crust out of the flour and shortening, a pie crust, if you please. This he fried in the little fry pans, covered one side with the fruit, then folded over the other side, making thereby a half-moon-shaped pie. He sold these pies for fifteen cents each or two for a quarter. At the end of five months when the grand jury met they failed to indict him and he was turned loose. When I checked him out he had paid me for what little I had advanced him and in addition had a total of ninety-seven dollars and seventy-five cents, just a little short of one hundred dollars. Here was a natural money-maker who saw an opportunity to make money and, of all places, in a county jail. Had Whitey's footsteps been turned in the right direction who knows how far he could have gone.

While I was still working for Del Lewis we received a reward circular showing the pictures of Butch Cassidy and Harry Longbaugh, stating that they had a few weeks previously held up a bank in Winnemucca, Nevada, and got away with $32,640. Del brought the circular in to me and asked about the two men; he knew I had punched cows with Cassidy. The picture of Cassidy was a good likeness; Longbaugh I did not know. I told Lewis that I did not know Longbaugh but that if he ever had to face

Cassidy to be sure to fire at the moment he called to him to throw up his hands or it would be too late, for Cassidy was double-geared lightning on the draw and a dead shot.

The story of Cassidy's loyalty was told me later by Will Carver who had been with McGinnis in the fight at Cimmaron Cienaga. It seems that Cassidy went to Santa Fe after the Winnemucca job and opened up negotiations to get McGinnis pardoned. I know nothing of how this was accomplished but McGinnis was pardoned. Butch Cassidy, after the pardon, refused to let McGinnis join with him and Longbaugh, telling him he had paid his debt and was now free and to keep it that way. I had often heard Cassidy say that he would give anything if he could be free again and this part of the story ties in with what Will Carver told me. Whatever you may think of a man engaged as Cassidy was in bank and train robberies, you have to admit he was not short on loyalty.

As time went on, a new sheriff was elected by the name of Stewart Hunt. I was to remain but in a subordinate position; this I agreed to do. We had a young Mexican boy, Chapo Eridio, condemned to be hanged for a murder which we all felt he never committed. As the hanging was to take place in about sixty days, the new sheriff was often congratulated upon his being elected just in time to perform this unpleasant task. A friend of mine heard Hunt say one day, as he was being kidded about the coming hanging, that he intended to delegate that job to me. When told this I immediately wired Clarence C. Chase who was general manager of the Greene Gold and Silver Company in Mexico for a job. Chase's answer was to report to him at Minaca Chihuahua as soon as convenient. I gave Hunt the customary notice and soon left for old Mexico to work for the Greene Company.

However, before leaving, I turned over to Chapo Eridio's attorney information about his case, and Eridio's sentence to be hanged was changed to life imprisonment. His being found guilty of killing Deputy Sheriff White was caused by the evidence given by Mrs. White when on the witness stand that, although the night was very dark, she was able to recognize young Eridio by the light caused when the smelter men dumped a load of hot slag over the slag dump. This she claimed lit up the scene and she said she saw Eridio with a Winchester at his shoulder kill White. Two smelter men who were working that night at the smelter said that Mrs. White was not telling the truth, that as soon as the shooting started, all the smelter men ran to take cover and no hot slag was dumped while the shooting was on. This was the evidence I provided and I am glad I was able to help little Chapo for I am certain he was absolutely innocent.

For this concession the Greene Company agreed to build a wagon road, 77 miles in length, which would connect the old Spanish mining camp of Ocampo with Temosachic, a town located on a branch railroad which was then building west out of Chihuahua. This road would open up a section of the country which for hundreds of years could only be covered by horseback.

The morning after my arrival at Minaca, Chase called me into the office and handed me a letter addressed to Mr. Phil Fall, a brother of A. B. Fall, who was one of Greene's attorneys at the time. Chase explained that at Casas Grandes some hundred miles southwest of El Paso, the company had about sixty saddle horses and wanted me to ride overland to Casas Grandes, ride out this string of horses and pick thirty-five head to be brought to Temosachic for the Greene Company's use. It seems that Greene had started a railroad out of Casas Grandes to run south to Temosachic but had stopped work after making better arrangements with the railroad then running to Minaca; they agreed to build a spur from La Junta to Temosachic, which had been done, so Greene stopped his railroad work at Casas Grandes.

I took a company bus which was then running from Minaca to Temosachic. Mr. Phil Fall met the bus and, as soon as I heard someone call him by name, I walked up to him and, introducing myself, handed him the letter. He opened it and read the message out loud, which stated that he was to furnish me with a horse and saddle, a pack horse and camping outfit and a *mozo*. I understood everything about the note except the *mozo* part; the nearest I could come to it was that I was to be furnished a Mauser rifle. The next morning Fall took me to the corral boss, a Jim Kane whom I had met in Arizona. Kane had already saddled the three horses, two with just saddles and one equipped with pack saddle and bags. I wondered about the third horse when Kane spoke up, "Axford, this bay is your horse, the sorrel is for your *mozo* who is familiar with the trail north," he then introduced me to a Miguel García. Kane told me to step over to the company store across the street from the corral and pick out what grub I would need for the trip. This was soon done and García and I started on our way.

Our first night's stop was made at the famous La Ba Victoria Ranch which was composed of about a million acres and was at that time owned by Mrs. Phoebe Hearst, the mother of William Randolph Hearst, the noted newspaper editor, and was in charge of a man by the name of Hays. This was the most beautiful ranch setting I had ever seen—an immense bowl-like place surrounded at the rim with heavy pine timber. As the rim broke into small ridges the trees changed from pine to oak, then the ridges flattened out into a gradually sloping plain heavily covered with grass. This plain was several miles in width and a number of bunches of cattle were seen grazing as we rode along. From a long distance away we could see the ranch house or hacienda gleaming white in the sunlight. I could see on approaching that this was no small outfit; the house was an immense affair with a large center court filled with beautiful flowers and shrubs. García and I dismounted and I approached the front where the sign read "Oficina"; as I reached the entrance a man quickly advanced to meet me, introduced himself as Mr. Hays and asked what he could do for us. I explained that I was working for the Greene Company and was on my way north to Casas Grandes after a bunch of saddle horses for the company and wanted to make arrangements to camp overnight, stating that I had my own camp outfit with me. Hays would not listen to my camping out, called a Mexican to take care of García and our horses and I went into the office with him. We sat and talked for a while, Hays stating he was glad to see Greene come into the country, saying "That's what Mexico needs—American capital to develop and open up this wonderful country." He further stated that the land had been purchased years ago by Senator Hearst for a few cents an acre, and that they were running about 40,000 head of cattle and a couple of bands of sheep. When he mentioned sheep he asked me if I had ever seen a $5,000 dog; my answer in the negative brought him quickly to his feet, "Come on, Axford, and I will show you a dog which we had shipped to us from Scotland; she was bred over there and has four puppies." We went out to the stables where Hays kept his team and saddle horses, and in a box stall was the little black mother with a white ring around her neck, surrounded by four puppies all with the same markings. We spent several minutes with the dogs, then Hays said we had better get back to the house as supper would soon be ready and remarked I would no doubt like to clean up a little. Going back to the house, Hays showed me to the room I was to occupy for the night. The room was simply furnished but had a good bed and a place to wash up. After supper Hays and I returned to his office and were busy until about midnight talking about our different experiences. The next morning as García and I were leaving, Hays asked me to be sure to stop in on our way back; I explained I would have about thirty-five head of horses with me when I returned. "That will make no difference; we have a small horse pasture to take care of your stock—you be sure to stop."

The trip north to Casas Grandes was over mountainous country and not very interesting until we started down a long canyon which, if my memory is correct, was called "Ruthio" canyon. This canyon had several signs of cliff dwellers in the bluffs on the canyon sides and had evidently been the home of cliff dwellers in the years long past. Upon reaching Casas Grandes I immediately found the engineer in charge of the Greene holdings, these consisting of Fresno scrapers, plowing equipment, a number of tents, picks and shovels, in addition to the horses. The next day we went out to a pasture and ran in the horses; it took a couple of days to ride out the bunch. I picked out thirty-five head and García and I started back, after making rope hobbles for all the horses, for we would have to hobble them each night to keep them from straying. We stopped again with Hays and, believe it or not, I talked him out of one of the $5,000 pups. He was the runt of the bunch. I made a bag out of a gunny sack and swung it by the saddle horn and carried the puppy that way.

After my return I was put to work under Steve Aguirre, the purchasing agent for the company, and it was my duty to load out the different wagons and pack animals with the supplies requisitioned by the different camps. Chase had moved his offices to Temosachic and the wagon road was already several miles out on its way to Ocampo, 77 miles away. I soon learned my duties, the company furnished a horse and I bought a Gallup and Frazier American saddle as I did not like the McClellan army saddles which they used. The wagon road continued to make good progress; we had a master of transportation by the name of Will Pomeroy. He often had information from the camps, which Aguirre's office did not have; for instance, a camp might be short of powder, and Pomeroy often had me unload a wagon which had been loaded, in order to take care of these emergency orders. This would offend Aguirre and Fred Reilly, his assistant, for they felt that Pomeroy was butting in where he did not have the authority, and as usual when one treads on the toes of another department, he is in for trouble.

Fred Reilly looked me up out on the job one day and advised me that Mr. Aguirre wanted me in the office, saying, "We have Pomeroy on the carpet in front of Chase and we want you to tell about the number of times we have had to change our loads on account of Pomeroy butting in." I walked to the office and found a very worried Pomeroy facing Aguirre and Mr. Chase. Aguirre had laid his complaint in front of Chase and was waiting for me to put on the finishing touches. Chase turned to me and asked me to tell my side of things. Reilly had said to me on the way to the office, "We've got that son of a b— where we want him and I am sure we will have a new master of transportation." I realized that here was a man being crucified on account of departmental jealousies, a man who only had the good of the company in mind when making these changes based upon information which he had and which had not been available to Aguirre's office. I got up and told them that in my mind the only mistake Pomeroy had made was in not taking the matter up first with Mr. Aguirre or Reilly, that I felt Will Pomeroy was a man dedicated to work for the best interests of the company at all times and had no intention of trying to run the mercantile department. "You will have to go a long way before you can find a better man to replace Mr. Pomeroy." With that statement out of my system I walked out of the office. I caught a smile on Chase's face as I went out the door. Fred Reilly followed me out, and said, "You have spoiled it all." "No, Fred, I have only improved things—from now on Pomeroy will work closer with your office." Pomeroy looked me up and thanked me for my statement, and from then on did work closely with Aguirre and Reilly and often went out of his way to help me when things got out of hand.

One morning while eating breakfast I was told that Mr. Chase wanted me in his office. He told me that he had borrowed me from Aguirre and wanted me to make a trip to the Sonora side of the Sierra Madre Mountains and get some mining-claim filing papers from one of their mining engineers whom I would find in a town by the name of Sauriripa. "I expect you to get over there and back in ten days. I have chosen you for this ride because I can depend upon you to get back here within the time limit and to bring the mining denouncements which are so necessary in order to hold our concession. These denouncement papers have to be in Mexico City by the last of the month." I had to ride day and night to get back in time but I made it.

Upon my return I was told to report to Scott White, the paymaster. He was getting ready to make one of his monthly trips (necessary) to pay off the men working on the wagon road which the Greene Company was building from Temosachic to Ocampo. Working on the road at the time were about two thousand Mexicans and a couple hundred Americans who had to be paid. As the payroll called for considerable cash, it was necessary to have armed guards accompany the paymaster. Johnny St. Clair, Sid Mullen and I were to accompany White, as guards.

The company had taken a number of old army McClellan saddles, had added skirt leathers and western stirrups and were using them instead of furnishing the higher priced western saddles. Scott White, Mullen, and I had our own saddles but St. Clair was riding one of the made-over McClellan trees. The McClellan saddle was the standard army saddle which had been used for years and was still in use by all cavalry units. The first day out St. Clair kept up with the group, but on the second day, would usually be riding about one hundred yards behind us and did not seem to be able to keep up. On the third day he was getting still further behind and Scott asked me what I thought was the matter, was he afraid or was he laying back, figuring if someone jumped us, he would be in a better position than if we were all bunched up. Scott sent me back to find out just what was the matter with St. Clair. I waited for Johnny to catch up and asked, "What's the matter—are you getting cold feet?" "Hell no!" said Johnny; "it's this damn saddle—no wonder it's used by the army. After riding this saddle for a few miles any soldier would get down and fight like a son of a b—." It was the hard riding in the old army saddle that caused Johnny to always be riding far behind.

After my return from this trip I was sent to Mesa Correo where the company had a warehouse and stage station. Mesa Correo was 9,500 feet high, on a mesa on top of the Sierra Madre Mountains; it was named Mesa Correo or Mail Mesa because years ago the Apache Indians had killed a Mexican mail carrier on the mesa.

The wagon road had been finished to Mesa Correo, a large warehouse and barn had been built, and I was to be the forwarding agent at that point and supply the different camps by pack burros and mules, which animals were supplied by Mexican packers who were hired for each trip. I remained at Mesa Correo several months. Soon the wagon road was finished to Concheno, the Concheno mine had been purchased by the company, and as the warehouse was not needed at Mesa Correo and the road was on its last lap to Ocampo, I was transferred to the mining department by Chase, and put in charge of the night shift at the Navidad mine, a new project where a

shaft was being put down on the vein adjoining the
Concheno mine. In addition to the shaft we were also
running a tunnel into the mountain to tap several surface
showings of ore which were higher up on the hill. In this
tunnel we had three shifts working, consisting of two
miners on each shift. I had just hired a new Mexican
miner and as the rock was hard it called for a good
double jack man to work in the tunnel. While on my way
from the shaft to the tunnel entrance, I was approached
by a Mexican who was holding a small glass bottle in his
hand. He introduced himself, saying that I had been
recommended to him as a good man and he was anxious
to have me look at the place where he had got the gold
which I could see in the little bottle. I examined the small
nuggets which showed in the bottle, about eight of them,
which looked more like filigree work as they were of
different shapes with many sharp fingers showing on the
specimens. I agreed to go with him to look over the
property as soon as I could make arrangements to get
away. As the trip, he said, would take about six days to
the property and back, it was necessary to arrange for a
saddle and a pack horse to make the trip. Gonzales had
his own saddle horse.

I got permission from C. C. Chase, the company
manager, and we were on our way. It was a two-
and-a-half day trip from Ocampo; we crossed the San
Tismo River through the little Mexican town of
Batapelas and up on a mountain called the San
Francisco; just above where the trail crossed what was
known as the San Francisco canyon, we came to a
lemon-yellow streak of decomposed material from
which the Mexican had got the nuggets. As we turned
off the trail Gonzales called my attention to places
which showed that years ago someone had done some
work. He said this was placer work which had been

done by San Francisco monks—hence the name of the mountain and canyon.

On the foot-wall side of the lemon-yellow deposit was a small seepage of water. Gonzales scooped out a basin for the water to settle in, took a tin plate from our utensils and, building a fire of brush, burnt the plate to get rid of any grease which might have been on it. When the basin was filled with water we proceeded to pan the yellow dirt and succeeded in getting several small nuggets; these were also like filigree work with sharp prongs on them; and another peculiarity, they were as bright and shiny as if they had just been made. As I knew only hardrock mining I did not understand what I was looking at, and on account of the nuggets being so clean and shiny, I got the idea that the Mexican had salted the deposit.

While the Greene Gold and Silver Company had a concession for five years which gave them the right to all minerals discovered during that period, this had no influence on my turning Gonzales down. It was my ignorance, not understanding what I was looking at, and my suspicion of the bright nuggets which looked to me as if they had just been made. Anyway, I returned to the Navidad mine and my job which I could understand, as a hardrock miner.

While working at the mine I was called to the phone one day and McDaniels, the chief clerk in the company offices in Temosachic, asked me if I knew a man by the name of George Rowland. Rowland had been a prisoner under me in Tombstone and had been sent to Yuma penitentiary for a period of one year. I happened to be on the same train that Rowland was on after he had served his time and was on his way back to Cochise County. Realizing that he had just got out and was no doubt broke, when I shook hands with him I left a ten-dollar bill in his hand. I had up to that moment when McDaniels called me to the phone had no knowledge of Rowland's whereabouts. My thought now was that Rowland had probably applied for a job and had given me as a reference. I told McDaniels that I knew a George Rowland. "Well, Axford, he has been working in the company sawmill at Sierra Madre and has a credit on the books of $475.00; he asked me to call you and tell you you can draw all or any part of it should you want to." This was truly bread cast upon the waters. I did not need the money but wrote Rowland to thank him for the offer.

Before I leave the Greene Gold and Silver Company I must tell you how Fred Reilly, Aguirre's assistant in the purchasing department, earned his nickname. Nicknames are sometimes just given and sometimes earned—this one was earned. It was about the year 1905 or 1906. Fred was considered a good judge of whiskey and often was taken to dinner by the many salesmen covering the territory. Fred did very well as a purchasing agent, driving many good bargains by which the company saved considerable money. We do not know for sure just which hardware salesman made the famous sale to Reilly but we do know that in due time a shipment of a thousand rat traps was received. Investigation showed a signed order by Reilly for the shipment.

Why, even in the year 1964, fifty-eight years later, I believe there were still Reilly rat traps in the company inventories. Needless to say, he earned his nickname "Rat-Trap Reilly."

When Friendship Called

While working as night shift foreman in the Concheno and Navidad mines then being operated by the Greene Gold and Silver Company I received a letter from Frank Moson, a son of Mrs. Greene by a previous marriage, asking me to come at once as he needed me to take care of a mining endeavor in which he was interested. I was rather reluctant to leave the company but on account of Moson's kindness to me while living with the Greene family, I felt that if he needed me he had the first call on my services.

A few days later I reported to Moson at Hereford, Arizona, where he was a part owner and superintendent of what were then the American interests of the Greene Cattle Company. I spent the night with Moson and his assay reports which showed the mine was producing ore having a value of $130 gold per ton, as Moson had related. Behan also showed me that the Alisos Mine owed the Montezuma Copper Company in Nacozari $5,130.00 Mexican money. This information made Moson extremely angry for he did not know about it and he again told me he would not put up another cent—would close down first. Moson and I went outside to talk things over; the mine was about five hundred feet farther up the hill from the camp. "Well, Moson, I will be frank with you; if it were anyone else but you I do not believe I would take the trouble to look at the mine, but let's go up and see what you have—maybe we can pull you out."

The mining foreman was a Swede named Martin Moe whom we met just outside on the waste dump at the tunnel entrance to the mine. On this dump Moe had four Mexicans busily sorting the ore, taking out the waste material. As the ore had to be packed twenty-five miles by burro and mule, only ore of course could be shipped. At the time Moe had about four hundred sacks of ore, which was about half a carload, already weighed and sacked. He took us inside, the tunnel had been driven into the hill for a distance of about one hundred ten feet; about sixty feet from the entrance was a rise from which the miners lowered the ore from the vein above by hand in rawhide buckets. He was overhead stoping, taking the ore down on heavy canvas to keep it as free from waste as possible. I quickly saw that as a miner Moe knew his business. We crawled up the ladder to look at the ore vein and found a vein running from two to three-and-a-half feet of good silver and lead ore. After the inspection we went outside and Moson immediately asked me for my decision. I agreed to stay and see what could be done. I insisted that Moson leave with me the horse and saddle, to which he agreed. The last words he said as he rode down the trail were, "Remember—not another cent; if you cannot make it pay, close her down."

That night I had a long talk with Behan and Moe. I found that the Mexican packers were being paid by the other miners in the district at the rate of thirteen dollars per ton Mexican money to pack the ore to Calabasas Station twenty-five miles away. Also learned that in a few days the payroll would have to be met and dynamite and commissary supplies purchased. The next morning I saddled up, told Moe to continue with the mine work and asked Behan to stay on a day or two as it was necessary for me to go in to Nacozari to talk with the Montezuma Copper Company officials. Somehow I had to arrange for the payroll and supplies to be taken care of. I was convinced I could make the mine pay if we could continue to operate.

When I arrived in Nacozari I rode immediately to the company store and asked for the manager, was taken into the office and met the manager, a Mr. McLaughlin. I introduced myself, told him what we had in the way of an ore body, what the ore assayed, and other pertinent facts, stating that our books showed that we owed them a little over five thousand dollars. I told Mr. McLaughlin what I would like him to do was to allow us to turn the ore over to him at Calabasas Station and have him ship it in his name until he had been paid what we owed him, adding further that it would be necessary, however, for him to take care of our payroll and supplies in the meantime. Mr. McLaughlin reached into a small index file sitting on his desk, drew out one of the cards, looked it over for a moment, then looked up saying his reports showed that what I said was true and that he would take care of our present needs. He pushed a button on his desk which called in one of the clerks and told him to supply me with payroll and commissary requisition blanks.

As I turned to leave after thanking him, he said he supposed I realized just what I was up against for animals to pack out the ore. With thirteen different mines trying to pack out ore, I would have to figure some way to keep my share of the Mexican packers. After my return I spent a little time meeting the different packers and learned that they were dissatisfied with the thirteen dollars payment per ton and wanted a raise. I met with them and agreed to raise the price for packing to fifteen dollars per ton. As the Alisos mine was the first mine in the district all the packers had to pass us on the way in. I told them that all I asked was that our ore be given the preference. When we had the ore ready for shipment I would wave them up the hill; if our ore was not ready they were to continue on to the other shippers.

We moved the camp from the bench above to the canyon floor which stopped the necessity of having to pack fuel and water up the hill and also put me in the position of being in the right spot to control the packers. I stopped the lowering of the ore in rawhide buckets by hand, punched a raise up to the ore about forty feet farther inside, boarded up the mouth and dropped the ore into this chute from where it was dropped into a mine car and rolled outside.

We paid off the Montezuma Copper Company, shipped several cars of ore for ourselves and later sold the property to a Los Angeles group. By taking on the job of getting the mine on a paying basis, I felt that I had helped pay back some of my early boyhood debts.

As soon as we had sold the Alisos Mine I was ordered by Moson to report to him at Hereford, the headquarters ranch of the Greene Cattle Company. A few months before I had read in one of the Bisbee papers about a strike on the Greene Cattle Company farm and how the strikers had run the superintendent off the ranch. When I met Frank he told me he wanted me to take charge of the Greene Cattle Company as superintendent.

When I took over the management of the company in 1907, one of the first things brought to my attention was the fact that the farm had never made a profit and was steadily showing a loss of about five thousand dollars per year. Range cattle always showed a profit, the company store a small profit, but the farm was always in the red. After three or four months of operation I realized that in order to find out where the leaks were I had to have a detailed breakdown from the company bookkeeper, showing me each month what it cost to run the store, the company boarding house, range cattle, headquarters residence and the farm. Charlie Work, the bookkeeper, was unable to give me the monthly report which was requested so I had the Cananea office send over a man. His first month proved he was not the man I wanted so I advertised in the Bisbee paper for a bookkeeper. One of the answers received was from a Walter Hodges who was one of the cashiers in a bank in Douglas. He seemed to be the best prospect so I wired him to come to Hereford the following weekend. Hodges arrived on the Saturday morning train and he and I sat down to talk things over. I explained the nature of the report I wanted and asked him if he could do the work. His reply was that he could give me what I wanted.

Hodges was about five feet nine in height and seemed rather thin, not weighing much over one hundred and thirty pounds. From his looks I got the idea that he was tubercular, so before closing with him I thought it advisable to talk it over with Hugh Fletcher, our store manager. I told Hugh, "This fellow says he can do the work but he seems to me to be a consumptive and as he will be working alongside of you, I want to know if this is agreeable to you before employing him. I would like to help this fellow, Hugh; furnish him a saddle horse and get him out into the open air." Fletcher's answer was a surprise—he stated he had come to Arizona years ago on a stretcher, down with consumption. "You bet I will work with him." Well, I hired Hodges; he remained in Douglas until the first of the month when he reported for work at our ranch. I gave him the list of monthly expense reports I wanted; cost of operating the boarding house per month, and cost per meal; cost of handling the range cattle, thoroughbred cattle, keeping our fences up; cost of operating the store, its purchases and sales, the headquarters residence and the farm; percentage of customer sales and company sales by the store.

The report that Hodges gave me was an eye opener. I found that when the range cattle outfit wanted wood hauled around to the different branding corrals, the farm furnished the labor, teams, etc., but that range cattle was never charged with the expenses. The farm was also furnishing labor to the store, in hauling its purchases from the depot to the store and warehouse, and for repairing fences when damaged, and hauling salt to the range. In fact, the farm was doing most of the work and range cattle, the store, and all the rest were not paying for any of this extra labor. Well, Hodges and I quickly changed all that; we kept track of this extra work done by the farm and made the farm show a profit. It was all a matter of bookkeeping.

I might here introduce you to a few of the men who were employed by the Greene Cattle Company.

Jim Kane, an ex-soldier, farm foreman
Hugh Fletcher, a good store man—store manager
Walter Hodges, a real office man—bookkeeper
Pink Murray, a top cowman—wagon boss
Jimmy Kane, Jr., a young cowboy, good hand with young horses
Jack Parker—cowboy
Jim Parker—cowboy

I had spent several days during my first few months in charge of the company visiting the different little cattle owners who always surround the bigger outfits. I found out, for some reason, there was some bad feeling against the company. I asked all to forget any feeling about the past, and to consider only my treatment of them while I was in charge. "I will treat you all square and I will ask the same treatment in return."

Among the many improvements being made by the company was the piping of water from springs in the Huachuca Mountains to troughs situated about three miles out on the flat. The reason for this was as follows. Between the San Pedro and the Huachuca Mountains to the west was a wide grassy plain about six or seven miles across. We found that our cattle watering either from the river or along the mountains were missing a strip of grass about two and a half miles wide in the middle. If we were to get any good from the grass, it would be necessary to either pipe water down from the mountains or drill a well and use windmills. We decided to pipe the water by gravity flow, filed a mining claim on what was known as the Lowry Springs. Jim Kane, our farm foreman, was to install the line and build the ground tank and troughs. We purchased the pipe and Kane proceeded with the work. We built a ground tank to control the flow by float valve into the troughs. Kane rode down to Hereford one day and advised that the work was finished and that the next day he would turn the water into the line.

A couple of days went by and I had commenced to wonder what had happened when Kane popped into the office all excited. "What's the matter, Jim?" I asked him. "Hell, I turned the water into the pipeline three days ago. Jack and I got on our horses and ran them all the way to the troughs so as to be sure to beat the water down. I have been camped there for over two days now and not a drop of water has come through." I drove into Tombstone to see my old boss, Master Mechanic Gordon, and explained the situation. Gordon explained that air pockets in the line kept the water from coming through; advised us to go over the line and tap in a number of stand pipes with a check valve in the top. This would release the air and also check the water. This was done and the water came through, proving that sometimes water will not run downhill.

worked several hundred miners and, as gambling was open, men often worked part time, first at mining to get a stake and then part time spent in gambling. This of course depended on the favors bestowed by Lady Luck, or how expert one was in handling a deck of cards. Ben Johnson was such a man. He was a big man physically, weighing in the neighborhood of two hundred pounds, and stood about six feet one in his stocking feet.

Ben had no doubt listened to stories often told about local cow men who had got their start by the use of a long rope and sometimes with the assistance of local cowboys who would steal the calves for a person at so much per head. With some such thought in mind Ben moved to the old Ninety Ranch lying in a little cove at the south end of the Huachuca Mountains. This ranch had been idle for a number of years and was open for anyone to take it up. Johnson had four or five cows and a couple of saddle horses, so was all set to go. The old ranch had a pasture of about sixty acres and had been fenced with a fairly good four-wire fence and boasted a three-room cabin and small shed which was used as a stable. The remainder of the ranch was government land. To make the picture complete, it is necessary to show the lay of the land surrounding the Ninety Ranch and what made it a perfect setup for the kind of operations which Johnson had mapped out for himself on his way to get rich. The international boundary line between Arizona and Mexico lay about two-and-a-half miles south of the ranch. This line was fenced for twenty-five or thirty miles with a good five-wire fence. On the American side was the Greene Cattle Company layout owned by Colonel W. C. Greene and his family, and on the Mexican side was the Cananea Cattle Company holdings also owned by Mr. Greene. While I was superintendent of the Greene Cattle

Company, Frank Moson was in charge of the Cananea Cattle Company holdings; in fact, he was also president of the Greene Company which made him my boss.

Johnson had been operating for several months and it had been reported to me that he was rustling unbranded calves so I had made a note that I must look over his range as soon as I could get time to do so. I also learned that he had made a statement that the Greene Cattle Company men had better stay clear of the Ninety Ranch unless looking for trouble, serving notice in a roundabout way that he considered himself a tough man to mix with. When riding the range opposite his ranch, the Cananea Cattle cowhands often rode over for a visit with their new neighbor. As mentioned before, the headquarters of the Greene Cattle Company were located at Hereford, which was on the railroad that ran from Benson to the town of Bisbee where the Copper Queen holdings were. The railroad ran straight through the company range, and at Hereford were located a large shipping pen and depot all under the supervision of a Mr. Holmes, the station master and telegraph operator. Holmes was also justice of the peace for that end of the county. The company holdings at Hereford consisted of a large headquarters residence, a company store and boarding house for employes of the farm part of the operations. The local post office was located in the company store building.

Frank Moson spent part of his time at Cananea Cattle Company offices but kept close tab on Greene Cattle Company operations by often using the mail service between the two places. One morning in going over the mail I found a letter from him addressed to me personally. In this letter he advised that Johnson had approached Cal Musgrove, a Cananea cowhand, and offered to give him five dollars per head for any unbranded calves. Musgrove reported this at once to Moson and they had fixed up a calf for Johnson by slipping a marked silver dime through a slit in the calf's hide just below the neck in the brisket part of the animal. This calf had been delivered to him two days before.

I was to swear out a warrant for Johnson and proceed to the Ninety Ranch taking along a couple of cowhands to help drive the cow and calf in to Hereford after arresting Johnson. Musgrove was to bring the cow with him and would meet us just below the Ninety Ranch. This called for quick action. I received this letter about eight in the morning and, as Musgrove was to meet us at noon and as the Ninety Ranch was about fifteen miles away, we had to get moving. I got Jimmy Kane and Jack Parker, two of my cowhands, to go along. I went over to the justice of the peace and swore out the warrant and we were on our way. Our ride to the Ninety Ranch took us over the Huachuca Flats up Montezuma Canyon to its head, with the ranch in the basin below. When we dropped off the mountain, Musgrove immediately joined us, stating that he had the cow tied up to a tree about two hundred yards below the ranch. We held a council to decide on our plan of operation, knowing that all depended on finding the calf first and it would also have to be branded by Johnson; if this was not done, we would have to wait until it was.

It was agreed that I would go to the house and engage Johnson in conversation; the boys were to round up his pasture and if the calf was found branded, one of them would ride up to the house to advise me. I would then serve the warrant. If the calf was found not branded, I was to spend about an hour with Johnson before leaving; the boys were not to show up. As I often rode by the Ninety Ranch on my way over to the San Rafael Ranch, it would not be unusual for me to make this little call.

The boys let down the wire at the back end of the pasture, crossed the horses through, and I rode on up to the house. In spite of the reports I had received I found Johnson very friendly—he invited me in and entertained me by showing some of his gambling equipment. Hardly ten minutes had passed until Jimmy Kane came riding up and looking over Johnson's shoulder when he opened the door informed me everything was all right. I immediately served the warrant on Johnson. At this point he got a little tough and asked how I intended to take him in. I had noticed a saddle horse in the shed already saddled when I rode up. I told him by horseback but he stated that under the law he had the right to demand a buggy. My answer was that I had seen men tied on a horse and taken in—how would he like that? "Oh! I'm going with you," he said, "I'm just telling you the law."

At this time he did not know that we had found the calf. I instructed Kane to get Johnson's horse from the shed and we stepped outside. The moment we stepped on to the porch Johnson saw the calf nursing the Greene Cattle Company cow which Musgrove had just brought up to join her calf. As I started to open the gate, telling the boys at the same time to drive the cow and calf outside and leave Johnson's other cattle inside, he made a grab for the gate. I shoved him away, ordered him to get on his horse and we were on our way. The three boys were driving the cow and calf and I was riding herd on Johnson. It was necessary to take the two animals before Holmes at Hereford as evidence in the case.

Riding alongside Johnson for several miles I tried to engage him in conversation but he would not talk. When we got in sight of Hereford I called Ben's attention to the fact and stated that after he had taken a drink or two in Hereford he would feel better. His reply was, "If I get to drinking, keep away from me, Axford; I am a very mean hombre when drinking." "Ben," I said, "I am the meanest son of a b— in Arizona when I am sober." No more was said and we rode into Hereford. He was immediately arraigned before Holmes, the evidence presented and he was bound over to await the action of the grand jury then in session at Tombstone. I suggested to Holmes that Ben be allowed to go on his own in order to return to his family which was then left alone on the Ninety Ranch. The grand jury indicted Johnson and a few days later found us all in Tombstone as witnesses in the case against him. We drove the cow and calf to Tombstone as evidence and figured we had a cinch case. The trial proceeded; Musgrove was first on the stand and told about Johnson offering him five dollars per head for unbranded calves, that he had reported this to his boss, Moson, and that a marked silver dime had been placed in the calf's brisket. Cunningham, Johnson's attorney, asked Musgrove if he had been paid for the calf. He replied that he had and produced the five dollar bill which was offered as evidence. Cunningham asked only this one question.

Moson followed Musgrove on the stand and corroborated the evidence of Musgrove as to the placing of the marked dime. Again Cunningham asked only one question. "You are the superintendent of the Cananea Cattle Company and also, I understand, president of the Greene Cattle Company, and as such, you had the proper authority to authorize Musgrove to deliver the calf to Johnson and accept five dollars in payment for same. Am I right?" Moson answered yes to this question. Cunningham then moved that the case be dismissed as it was an authorized and legal sale.

The rest of us, Kane, Parker and I, were never called. The cow and calf were on the courthouse lawn also ready for testimony. The five-dollar bill was offered to Mr. Moson who refused it saying it did not belong to him. Johnson was instructed by his attorney not to claim the bill. When I last saw it, it was lying on the clerk's desk— an orphan which no one would claim. The charge against Johnson was dismissed. The crime was legal.

However, my duties as deputy sheriff were easy to take care of; once in a while something happened such as the time I had to arrest a woman for attempted murder. Grossman was in charge of a copper mine in the upper part of Ash Canyon located on the east slope of the Huachuca Mountains in Cochise County. The mine employed about ten men who were engaged in sinking a shaft on the property. When down to a depth of seventy-five feet they ran into some water and a pumping plant was necessary in order to keep the water down so the shaft could proceed.

In addition to the mining crew Grossman employed a Mrs. Sullivan as cook in charge of the boarding house. It seems that for some reason her services were not satisfactory so Grossman, unknown to her, intended to replace her with a Chinaman as cook. He had the cook sent out from Tombstone and he arrived by Fletcher's stage just before dark. Grossman, taking the Chinaman with him, entered the dining room and advised Mrs. Sullivan that he was replacing her with the Chinaman. I do not know just what went wrong with Mrs. Sullivan at the moment but I found Justice of the Peace Holmes waiting for me when I came riding down early the next morning. I was living on the Martin place about a mile south of Hereford and usually rode down each morning to have breakfast with Mrs. Parker who ran the company boarding house, so as to be on top of things early in the day. When I saw Holmes standing in the road in front of the depot and apparently waiting for me I knew something was wrong. Holmes' first action was to hand me a paper which I immediately recognized as a warrant for arrest. "What's this, Holmes?" I asked. "It's a warrant for a Mrs. Sullivan, the cook at Grossman's mine," and he proceeded to fill me in on the facts. It seems that when Grossman with the Chinaman trailing him had advised Mrs. Sullivan of her dismissal she immediately rushed into her bedroom which adjoined the dining room, came out with a pistol in her hand and commenced shooting. Whether she shot to kill I do not know but she missed both Grossman and the Chinaman as they rushed outside, but she followed them firing a couple more shots as they fled.

Grossman had walked down to Hereford during the night and had sworn out a warrant for the arrest of Mrs. Sullivan for attempted murder. "My God! Holmes, this is a woman, and evidently, from what you say, a crazy woman; this is a tough job for anyone." I talked with Grossman who was still a very excited man. He stated that about four shots had been fired by Mrs. Sullivan and he considered he was very lucky to be alive. As deputy sheriff, if I arrested Mrs. Sullivan I would have to transport her to Hereford. I had a double seated hack hitched up, arranged to have Jack Parker drive the rig, and asked Grossman if he wanted to go along. He refused to go, saying there was not enough money in Arizona to get him to go back as long as Mrs. Sullivan was still on the loose.

Parker was instructed to pull out for Ash Canyon while Jimmie Kane and I rode ahead on our horses. Kane and I talked the matter over on the way up. I told Jimmie that I had never arrested a woman and that one with a gun might prove to be somewhat of a problem. If she refused arrest and pulled her gun, just what to do was the question to be solved. Knowing the story from Grossman,

I told Jimmie that when we go in one of us must place himself between Mrs. Sullivan and her bedroom. We arrived at the mine about one o'clock in the afternoon and went immediately to the boarding house where we were met by Mrs. Sullivan in a very pleasant way. I asked her if we were too late for dinner; she said, "No, come in and I will get something ready for you." We went in and sat down at the table while Mrs. Sullivan busied herself in the kitchen. The bedroom door was open and I could see a large trunk and a dresser of some kind through the open doorway.

Our meal was served and as we arose from the table, I stepped between Mrs. Sullivan and the bedroom and told her I had a very unpleasant task to perform. I served the warrant on her, telling her she was under arrest for attempted murder. I do not believe I have ever met a more pleasant person, about forty-five or fifty years of age and I was rather amazed that she could have gone berserk as Grossman had stated. She denied everything, said she did not even own a gun, and a complete search of the trunk which she had packed and ready to go did not turn up any weapon. Parker had arrived with the rig, we loaded Mrs. Sullivan and her trunk aboard, tied Kane's horse on behind and I instructed him to ride with the others in the hack, that I intended to look around a little but would overtake them before they got out of the canyon.

I could hear someone using an anvil, evidently sharpening tools, from the blows being made, so I walked up the canyon where I found a blacksmith shop and a man busily engaged in sharpening drills. I asked him about the shooting. He said, "It is true—I guess Mrs. Sullivan was aroused because Grossman had brought in a Chinaman to relieve her." "Is the Chinaman here?" I asked. "Yes, I will call him and you can ask him about the shooting."

The Chinaman, still excited, said that she fired several shots at 'him and Grossman and wanted to know if she was still there. I told him I had arrested her and was taking her to Hereford and that he had better get into the kitchen and prepare the evening meal for the men. He at first refused but I finally convinced him that he would have to do the cooking until other arrangements could be made.

I rode down the canyon and overtook the rig, exchanged with Kane and, getting into the rig, explained to Mrs. Sullivan that she was up against a long prison sentence, that the evidence of Grossman, the Chinaman and some of the miners who witnessed the shooting would certainly convict her. She still maintained she had done no shooting. Just before we got to Hereford she asked how she would be tried and I told her first before Justice Holmes the next morning. She then gave me a list of ten men working at the mine, stating she wanted subpoenas made for all ten. Sensing that this would shut down the mine and stop the pumping, I told her I might get Grossman to dismiss the charges—at least I would try.

That evening I talked with Grossman and asked him just how much damage it would cause him if all the crew was subpoenaed from the mine and the shaft allowed to fill up with water. He said the shutting down of the mine would cause him considerable damage. The dollar sign overcame his desire to prosecute and he agreed to drop the charges if Mrs. Sullivan would take the train out of the country. She left on the morning train, Grossman went back to Ash Canyon, and I still consider myself lucky with my first and only arrest of a woman.

And again, you never can tell who and what will make trouble. The following story will tell you of our difficulties with United States soldiers. Fort Huachuca, one of the United States Army Posts in what was then Arizona Territory, was occupied by the Sixth Cavalry under the command of Major Allen. The Fort consisted of the usual parade ground, faced on the east side by four or five residences for the officer personnel, and on the west side by three or four long barracks buildings, the usual kitchen and dining room, the guard house or fort jail, and further west the barns, stables and corrals. Fort Huachuca was located on the northwest end of the Huachuca Mountains. At that time it was unfenced and open range, although later on the expanded military reservation, was well fenced all the way around.

The Greene Cattle Company range surrounded the fort on all sides and its cattle often grazed right up to the fort itself which was well fenced. Almost every year our cowhands, in riding in the vicinity of the fort, had found where one or two cattle had been butchered, the meat taken away and only the hide and head left behind. We were sure this meat was being taken into the fort, but were baffled by a lack of motive, as the government furnished all food supplies and we could hardly believe that the soldiers were doing the killing. There was however a Chinaman operating a restaurant inside the fort premises and we felt that somehow the Chinaman was the one to benefit. The situation called for a close inspection to be kept at all times, any wagon tracks leading from the fort to be trailed out to their end and their mission firmly established if possible. We ran out the destination of several wood wagons but had no luck otherwise.

Pink Murray, our wagon boss, had moved his outfit into what we called the Big Tank and was busy combing the range for all company steers, one, two and three years old, to be delivered to a California buyer by the name of Hall with whom we had contracted to deliver not less than one thousand head. The pay we received for these steers in 1907 may be of interest, for the prices were sixteen dollars for yearlings, eighteen-fifty for two-year olds and twenty-one dollars for full three-year olds. The Big Tank was located about five or six miles east of the fort and just outside the military reservation. Water had been piped down from a spring in the foothills above to the ground tank and from the tank to a battery of wooden water troughs controlled by a float valve which would shut off the water when the troughs were full.

In rounding up early one morning, Murray came across a freshly killed beef with only the hide and head left. This time there was this difference—the tracks of a two-wheeled cart were plainly visible leading towards the fort. Murray dropped rounding up and together with Fred Bennett trailed the tracks right into the fort and found the beef in Troop C's icebox. The excited cook blurted out the names of three soldiers who had brought in the beef. Murray sent one of his men with a note to me, at our Hereford headquarters, stating the circumstances and giving me the names of these men. I have forgotten them now but for the purpose of our story it will make no difference. The station master, Holmes, had been made the justice of the peace for our district to enable us to get quick action in case of trouble and I had been made a deputy sheriff for the same reason. Immediately upon getting the note from Murray, I walked over to the depot and swore out grand larceny warrants for the three soldiers. This was still in the morning hours of the same day that Murray found the killed beef. I wired the district attorney in Tombstone, giving full particulars and asked him if it was possible to arrest these men on government property or would I have to catch them off the reservation before serving the warrants. He advised that civil law was superior and I could arrest the men right on the fort. I then asked him to have the head deputy, Porter McDonald, meet me in Fort Huachuca at two o'clock that afternoon. Some of you will remember Porter McDonald, for he picked up Aimee Semple Mc-Pherson just east of Douglas in her famous kidnapping case years ago. Anyway, Porter was afraid of no man and I wanted him along in case I experienced any trouble in getting the men out of the fort. Arranging for a team and hack to follow, the hack being necessary to bring the prisoners to Hereford to be tried before Justice Holmes, we started for the fort.

Fort Huachuca was only about thirteen or fourteen miles from Hereford, so mounting a fast horse and with the warrants in my pocket, I set out. Arriving at the fort just at two o'clock I looked for McDonald but he had evidently not arrived. I knew Major Allen was in charge so I asked to be taken to him. I was directed to one of the officers' residences in front of which I could see the Major's orderly walking up and down. I rode up, ground-hitched my horse and introduced myself to the orderly who announced me to Major Allen. Relating my mission to him, I was invited to sit down and explain more thoroughly. He offered me a Manila stogy and I told him about the killing of our beef which had been going on for years and how anxious we were to stop it. He said he had been expecting me and that he had two of the soldiers wanted in the guard house. About this time I heard Porter ask the orderly in front where the rider of the horse was. Some of you oldtimers may remember Porter and how he talked through his nose and was not a man who whispered his words. I am sure everyone in Fort Huachuca heard Porter at the time. He came inside and met the Major, who gave an order for the men to be turned over to us.

When we received the men they asked what was to be done with them. I explained that they were to be taken to Hereford and tried before Justice Holmes the next morning and if held over for the grand jury would be taken to the county jail in Tombstone to await their action. By this time the hack had arrived from the ranch. The prisoners asked if they could take a change of clothes, tobacco and the like with them; I agreed and we went into one of the barracks buildings to get their belongings. About this time a couple of soldiers asked to speak to me and pleaded for me to let the missing soldier go, stating that he was a fine fellow and was to be married in a few days. I listened to their appeal, but made no answer to the request at the time.

The barracks was an immense building—I should judge at least eighty feet in length. In the center was a line of gun racks in which the guns were locked; a soldier with a dust rag was at the time unlocking one gun at a time and wiping it off with an oily rag. On each side were the beds of the soldiers. While our prisoners were collecting the things desired, a group of soldiers came rushing in and asked what we meant by trying to arrest United States soldiers on government property. There were, as I remember, six men in the group and seemed to be led by a big redheaded, red-faced trooper who appeared tough. This redhead walked up to the soldier dusting of the guns and ordered him to hand over the key to the gun rack and they'd see if the soldiers could be taken. Porter motioned to me to step back a little which I immediately did; this put the six soldiers between us. Porter then looking the redhead straight in the eye said, "Give the son of a b---- the key to the gun rack." They took one good look at the setup, saw we had them between us, and turned around and walked out. The rig was waiting outside for the prisoners and we started for Hereford.

The trial was set for ten o'clock the next morning; at about nine-thirty a government rig arrived with five men in charge of a first lieutenant who advised Holmes he had been appointed to defend the prisoners. I do not know how things of this nature spread, but when time for the trial arrived we had a fair-sized group of ranchers and cowhands to listen to the trial. The lieutenant depended altogether on the premise that there was not a motive for soldiers to kill beef to bring into the fort as all food was provided by the government. Just before the trial opened I overheard several ranchers talking when the same question was raised—why steal beef when the government paid the food bill. In answer to this one of the men spoke up—"Hell, I'll tell you—I used to be in the Army. The Army allots to each company a budgeted list of rations and if the soldiers can save on the list, they are allowed to put this savings into what they call a 'Smoker Fund' to be used for entertainment purposes."

This overheard conversation covered the case. We proved the existence of the Smoker Fund which was the motive which had us baffled for so long. The two soldiers were bound over to await action by the grand jury. As they met only twice a year, several months could pass before a case could be settled and in the absence of bail a prisoner would have to remain in custody for that period. In a couple of months, the District Attorney's office in Tombstone was pressured by a General Bliss in charge of the Western Military Division to turn the soldiers over to the Army who wanted them to join the Sixth Cavalry in the Hawaiian Islands; he promised the Army would punish the men. As we were more interested in stopping the killing of our beef than punishing the soldiers, I finally agreed to a dismissal of the charges and the soldiers were sent on to join their company. Whether or not the government ever punished these men I have no way of knowing.

Still With the Greene Cattle Company

With the exception of one or two small cowmen I found the Greene Cattle range comparatively free from calf rustling. The owner of a ranch on the Barbocomari was giving us some trouble, so I told Pink Murray that when the roundup started on the head of the Barbocomari, this rancher was not to work with the wagon. I had been pleading with the man for several months to stop his stealing of our calves and to go straight. This he had promised to do, but then we followed him when he was delivering a bunch of beef cattle to a cattle buyer in Tombstone, and found three large calves supposably tied up on his trail to Tombstone, this was too much, so I had him barred from working with our wagon. Murray got cold feet and sent word to me that he wanted me there the first morning the roundup started to work as he expected trouble.

The work started at the old Tom Turner ranch and was to work north down the Barbocomari. I arrived at the Turner place just in time for supper the evening before. It seemed that the rustler had asked John Yost to look after his interests and Yost had some reputation as a fighter. We started our drive just at daybreak and shortly after sunup had a herd of about four hundred and fifty head of cattle rounded up. Everything was working fine; the fellow did not show up and the boys were patiently working the cows and calves out of the herd to be taken to corrals where the calves would be branded.

I was on the opposite side of the herd, away from the cut, when I heard loud, rough language on the cut side and I plainly heard John Yost tell someone that no Greene Cattle Company employee was going to cut out that cow. I rushed to the other side of the herd and found Yost facing Murray. It seems that a calf with the brand in question was nursing a red roan company cow and that Yost had turned the cow back and would not let Murray cut her out to the cow and calf cut which the boys were holding. Yost turned to me and repeated that no company employee was going to take that calf; that it belonged to his boss. The cow and calf had gone back into the herd; I asked Murray to point her out to me and saw the calf nursing one of our cows, which was all I wanted. Riding back to Yost, I told him that I was cutting the cow and calf out of the roundup and for him to get between the roundup and the cut and try to stop me if he thought he was man enough. I brought the cow and calf out past Yost and he made no move to stop me.

We had finished working the roundup, and the boys were on their way to the corral where the calves would be branded. I had stopped to cinch my saddle and was loping to overtake the boys when I found John Yost riding slowly with his head down, about a hundred yards behind the boys. I slowed down to a walk and started telling him how badly I felt about having to call his hand over the cow and calf deal, and said I had no hard feelings over the matter. John said, "But darn it, Axford, that calf does belong to my boss." He said it originally belonged to a crippled old cow which died in a bog and the calf took up with the company cow. He said, "Henry Piatt knows the calf and will tell you I'm telling you the truth." "Well, John," I told him, "if Henry Piatt tells me that the calf belongs to your boss, you will get it, for the company does not want anything that does not rightly belong to it. Piatt is up ahead—let's lope up and see him." Well, Piatt confirmed Yost's statement about the calf. "John," I said, "if you had told about this in the first place instead of trying to force your way, this could all have been avoided." The right man got the calf; we let it remain with the cow, branding a stripe on its neck to show just which brand belonged on the calf. Yost took the wrong way to accomplish his purpose.

In the early days western cattlemen were not bothered by homesteaders looking for land to file on, but lately several filings had been made in the valley, so it was necessary to go over your holdings and protect yourself on lands open for entry in which you yourself were interested. Adjoining the Greene Cattle land holdings on he south were one hundred and sixty acres, mostly river bottom land, which straddled our irrigation ditch coming from a dam on the San Pedro River which the Greene interests had built some years before. This 160 lay between the company land and the Sneed place which was also owned by the company and had lain open for years for anyone to homestead.

Arizona had started to grow, and many settlers were coming to this new western territory, so, in order to protect the land, the company had placed Hyde and Benson land scrip on the 160 acres. We were advised by the company attorney that the Hyde and Benson scrip legality was in question, so we talked Uncle Jimmy Martin, who was a distant relative of Mrs. Greene, into homesteading the 160 acres. Uncle Jimmy was bothered a lot with a rheumatic condition which caused the old man to be cranky and hard to get along with. He kept wanting the company to build him a better house; he had built a two-room shack on the premises and thought on account of his being related to Mrs. Greene that she was mistreating him, because the company refused to build. While Uncle Jimmy had a squatter's right, the Hyde and Benson scrip still held a prior right. Uncle Jimmy, getting madder and madder, one day sold his rights to two brothers named Jackson and left for his prior home in California. When the brothers found out that the property was in the courts, they sold whatever rights they had to a Mr. Miller and his boy, Roy.

On account of Hereford having the only shipping pens in the vicinity, the company had always kept a wide lane between its fences to allow the driving of large herds of cattle to the stockyards. One morning several weeks after Miller and his son had moved in, I saw them busily digging post holes on a line which would narrow the wide lane so necessary for our operations; so I rode up to explain to Miller that the land was still in dispute and to ask him to delay his fencing until the courts decided just who would get the property. When I rode up, old man

Miller had an axe in his hand and was busy cutting some low sage out of his proposed fence line. I asked him to stop building the fence until—this was as far as I got. The old man raising his axe came charging at me, swinging the axe. I jumped the horse to one side, held up my hand and said, "Dad, I don't want to hurt you; if you will not listen to reason and must make a fight of it, turn it over to your boy." "No," Miller said, "you might hurt the boy but you can't cheat me out of many years, so it's our fight." I was armed at the time and his boy was armed; however, he did not join in, letting the old man do all the talking. Keeping out of reach of the axe, I told Miller to talk to a lawyer, but to stop fencing until he had the right to fence. I explained why we kept a wide lane, in order to pass our cattle through. I rode back to the store and looking out about an hour later I noticed that the fencing had been stopped.

Several months after, the case still had not been settled and riding by one day, Miller flagged me down. He told me he guessed he would have to give up, his money was exhausted, and he apologized to me for his actions with the axe, stating further that if his boy could get work maybe he could make it. I told Miller to send his boy up and I would give him a job and if he needed credit at the store it would be given. I worked young Miller for several months; in the meantime the Hyde and Benson scrip won out and Miller and his boy returned to their home somewhere in Colorado. However I will always remember what Miller said, "You might hurt my boy, but you can't cheat me out of many years." One thing I have learned in my numerous years is to be careful when dealing with a young boy as his emotions are not under control and he explodes easily while an old man will figure you can't cheat him out of much anyway—so here goes.

We often had eastern people write and want to come out to spend a little time at the ranch; the year before we had George Patulla, a short story writer and also Irwin E. Smith, a photographer from Boston, who wanted to take pictures of what he called the passing type of cowboy. We enjoyed both of these boys very much, so when a fellow by the name of Kibbey wrote and asked for permission to come out, I had Hodges, the bookkeeper, write him to come on. In due time Kibbey arrived—he was not exactly what we expected him to be. Coming from Boston we were prepared for a young man with eyeglasses—he had to have glasses to go with the high-forehead, teacher-type of person we imagined him to be.

We knew Kibbey was coming on a certain morning so I strolled over to the depot to give him a welcome to Arizona. A square-built young man weighing around a hundred and seventy-five pounds, about five feet ten in height, came rushing off the train, with his baggage tickets already in his hands, and headed for Holmes, the station master. I started to turn away, thinking Kibbey is not on this train, when I heard him boom out to Holmes, "I am Kibbey and am looking for the Greene Cattle Company headquarters ranch." "Well, Kibbey," said Holmes, "there she is," waving his hand toward the company store and the headquarters residence, both of which were about three hundred feet away, in plain sight. For a moment Kibbey was stopped in his tracks, surprised to find that as soon as he had stepped off the train he was already at headquarters.

By this time I had reached him and, introducing myself, welcomed Kibbey to Arizona. He grabbed my extended hand and bearing down with all his hundred and seventy-five pounds of muscle, made me glad to get loose from this exceptionally healthy young man from Boston.

I helped Kibbey gather his gear and took him over to the store, introduced him to Hodges and Fletcher, and then started to take him over to a room we had reserved for him in the headquarters residence. He said he did not want a room—he came out to rough it and wanted to go to the chuck wagon and stay with the boys. What a different type from Boston Kibbey proved to be. He was green but a more willing worker never existed; he would get on anything, be thrown off, get up and try it again. In no time he had won the friendship of the boys and before the spring work was over was better than the average cowhand in his work. He had brought along a kodak and was always busy taking pictures as he went along.

I had just taken over the management of the San Rafael Ranch for the company, in addition to looking after the Greene Cattle Company spread. San Rafael was owned by the Cananea Cattle Company which also was owned by Colonel Greene. The San Rafael was a show ranch recently purchased from Colin Cameron who had made a grand effort to make a show place out of it. The fenced part of the ranch consisted of about twenty-two thousand acres of grass lands in the valley between two mountain ranges. The ranch house had been built on one of the higher elevations; here, in addition, was the main corral with all pastures leading into the large corral like the spokes in a wagon wheel. If you have ever seen the picture "Oklahoma," you will have some idea about San Rafael, for it was filmed on this ranch.

Anyway, in addition to several hundred head of thoroughbred Hereford cattle, there were about thirty-five or forty head of Shetland ponies, in one of the pastures. I wanted to look over these ponies and pick out several of them to be taken to Hereford where I intended to turn them over to a bunch of boys ranging from fifteen years down to eight, to be broken by them to the saddle. I had told the boys what I wanted to do with the Shetlands, and the kids were rarin' to go, and kept after me to bring them over. As the Mosons were going over with me, we thought we had better take Kibbey along—it would give him a chance to take pictures of some of the thoroughbred white-faced cattle and the Shetlands. So, we took Kibbey along.

We arrived at San Rafael and early the next morning I had the boys bring the Shetlands in, as I was anxious to look them over and pick out the ones for the kids at Hereford to break to ride. We heard the boys drive the ponies in while we were just finishing our breakfast. Kibbey jumped up from the table, picked up his camera and told Mrs. Moson that he wanted his picture taken on one of the Shetlands and explained to her just what to do in taking the picture. It seems there was a pinto stallion in the bunch which no man could ride bareback; you could weigh him down with a saddle and make it, but to get on him bareback was impossible, for the moment you raised your leg to get on, the stallion jumped right into you a-bucking, and bowled you over. Moson, who knew about the pinto, asked Kibbey if he would not prefer a pinto for his picture. I knew nothing about the horse but could sense that something was in the making, so I added my voice in favor of the pinto. The boys had been tipped off and already had him ready with a bridle on but no saddle. Kibbey spent a little time getting ready; he stationed Mrs. Moson with her back to the sun and told her to allow him time to get on the horse before snapping the picture. Everything was ready, Kibbey raised his leg to mount and the pinto barged into him, a-bucking. Mrs. Moson got the picture with Kibbey on the ground and the little pinto standing over him.

Kibbey spent several months with us and after his return to Boston sent us prints of the pictures he had taken. I noticed he had omitted to send the picture of the pinto, so I had Hodges write him a letter of thanks saying that what we wanted most, however, was the picture of him riding the pinto stallion at San Rafael. Kibbey's answer contained only one line: "You can go to hell."

Sometimes some amusing things took place; this little event was brought about by a cowhand's method of getting rid of an electric light globe. I had ridden into Nogales from the San Rafael Ranch under instructions from Colonel W. C. Greene to meet and get acquainted with a Mr. W. H. B. Kent, a Forest Service ranger who was coming to replace the present supervisor of the Garcia National Forest Reservation. As the reservation covered a substantial portion of our range we were of course anxious to meet the new supervisor and offer any assistance needed in going over our problems with the reservation rangers. These problems had not been settled satisfactorily with the outgoing supervisor and led to his replacement by Mr. Kent.

I checked in at the Montezuma Hotel which was then owned and operated by the Santa Rita Hotel interests in Tucson. I met Mr. Kent and after spending most of the afternoon in consultation with him, returned to the hotel where I found Henry Piatt, a cattleman and neighbor of ours who was also running cattle on the reservation. I found he was having trouble getting a room for the night as the hotel had no vacancies. I invited him to share my room and he gladly accepted my offer. After supper we sat in the lobby, Piatt and I, talking over what we thought should be added to our complaints about the Forest Reserves operations.

About nine o'clock Piatt stated he was rather tired from his ride and thought he would turn in. I took him up to the room, turned on the electric light from a switch on the wall; as this light was on the length of a cord it was necessary to show him how it operated. He evidently missed seeing me use the switch on the wall. There was no switch on the globe. On account of mosquitoes the bed was completely covered with a canopy of mosquito netting and the long cord enabled one to take the light under the canopy with him. Leaving Piatt propped up in bed looking over a magazine, I left, supposing that all was well. About eleven o'clock I went up to my room, turned on the switch but had no light. I woke up Piatt and asked him what had happened to the light. "I put the damn thing in the top bureau drawer and shut the drawer—I couldn't find out how to put it out." I could see a small line of light at the top of the drawer, so pulled it out and took out the light which was still lit. Anyway it was years before Piatt forgot about his way of turning off an electric light, for he sometimes was called by the boys "Bureau Drawer Piatt."

There's another little incident that lingers in my memory—when Ed Tovrea made two purchases of stock, one of cattle and one of hogs. One he wanted to talk about—the other he did not want to mention. In the early 1900's the Greene Cattle Company was a pardner of Tovrea in a butcher shop in Bisbee. In later years he made the Tovrea Meat Company into a multi-million dollar enterprise. Ed was known in early years as the best poker player in Arizona, a fact attested to by many an old-time gambler. At the time of this story cattlemen were commencing to get tired of selling cattle by their ages and were trying to make a market where cattle would be bought and sold at so much per pound, instead of as 1-year, 2-year, and 3-year olds.

Tovrea had contacted Moson, the president of the company, and wanted twenty-five 3-year olds delivered on a certain date, at $25.00 per head, the prevailing price for three-year olds. I was instructed to have the steers weighed out and to insist on their being weighed. Ed did not like the idea of selling them by the pound and, looking the steers over, said, "Axford, I'll give you $26.00 a round." This was $1.00 above the regular price. As my instructions were to weigh them out I stood by my guns and Tovrea weighed them and they brought not quite $24.00 per head, or $2.00 less than offered. Ed had a lot of fun over this sale and advertised it high and wide, how he had put it over on Moson and Axford on the deal.

W. C. Greene had in mind starting a packing plant in Cananea and during the summer had shipped out about two hundred head of Berkshire hogs from Iowa with instructions to run them on the alfalfa field at Hereford. We had been advised earlier about the hogs coming and had fenced a part of our alfalfa into five and ten acre tracts, fencing with good heavy hog wire. The hogs increased and prospered, but the first winter the bunch took sick with what is known as Swine Plague, a malignant form of pneumonia and we commenced to lose them. I sent for the territorial veterinary who looked the herd over. I had three pens—sick, very sick, and damn sick—when a hog reached the damn sick pen he was destroyed and the body burned. We lost over half of our herd before spring.

That spring Ed Tovrea came by and looked over the bunch of very thin hogs and stated we were lucky to have saved as many as we did. The hogs that were left, about

240 head, were soon in alfalfa up to their sides and amazingly took on flesh very rapidly. They looked so good that I told Jim Kane, our farm foreman, to butcher one for the boarding house. Kane picked one out, had it butchered and found that its lungs seemed badly damaged, had several chalky white spots in them. He came up to the office and told me I had better take a look. There was nothing wrong with the meat, but the lungs had been so badly scarred, that I quickly saw another winter would probably take the whole herd. I instructed Kane to kill another hog and if its lungs showed the same spots to let me know. He reported that its lungs were also affected. I wrote the veterinary about this and he advised that the meat was all right for human consumption but that I had better dispose of the herd before the winter months.

I immediately hopped the train to Bisbee to see Tovrea, told Ed that I wanted to sell him the entire herd of 240 hogs. Tovrea had seen them earlier when they were very poor and figured he could make some money on the deal. He asked me what I wanted for the bunch and I told him he could have them for 5 cents per pound. "Wait a minute," said Ed and, grabbing the phone, got in touch with the C & A farm foreman and asked him if he could handle the hogs on the alfalfa at the ranch. The foreman replied that he could take care of them. Ed said he would take the bunch, to ship them to Don Louis Station, have the hogs weighed in by the C & A foreman, bring the weights to me and I would get the money. I immediately ordered a car set in at Hereford, instructed Kane to take a couple of men with him, have the hogs weighed in at Don Louis, get the C & A Farm foreman to okay the weight, take it to Tovrea, get a check from him and deposit it in the bank immediately

A Threatened Range War

Old Charlie who ran his cattle on the head of
Government Draw on the divide between Sulphur Springs
Valley and our range on the San Pedro River had been
having some trouble with the 4-Bar outfit and the first
thing I knew a report was brought to me by our cowboys
Kane and Glenn that Charlie's outfit had thrown about a
thousand head of cattle into our lower range. I knew that
Charlie had been having some trouble with the 4-Bar
outfit and had been barred from working with the 4-Bar
wagon. It seems that Charlie had two or three thousand
head of cattle and when the 4-Bar outfit, in working the
range, often found they had to brand several hundred of
Charlie's calves, Charlie would have only one man to
represent him with the 4-Bar wagon. Even after repeated

requests from the 4-Bar, Charlie still refused to hire his share of men when working his range. So the 4-Bar not only barred him from its roundup wagon, but also commenced to line-ride Charlie's cattle, running them away from 4-Bar watering places.

I had talked with Billy Neal who was running the 4-Bar outfit and understood the situation, and it worried me considerably. The Greene Company owned several thousand acres of land extending about twelve miles up and down the San Pedro and about three miles in width. The railroad from Benson to Bisbee ran straight up through this land and openings had to be left for stock to pass through to water, under the Arizona law.

I made a hurried trip to see our lawyer in Tombstone. Young Doan advised that as we owned the land we could fence these water gaps in the railroad fence, providing we did not tie directly into the railroad fence, putting the fence about one foot away and then fencing straight across. I immediately started Joe Cross with a couple of farm hands down to do this fencing. The next day he came rushing back to the ranch, stating that Charlie and two of his men had ridden up heavily armed, had roped and pulled out the fence posts and warned him to see that the fence was not replaced. As Charlie's ranch was only about ten miles away, I called a man I'll refer to as Jay Smith and gave him a note which I asked him to deliver to Charlie's ranch. In this note I told Charlie that I was sorry I was not there to receive him when he tore out the fence but that it would be repaired at once and as he had three men to do the job I would also have three men to meet him when he rode in. "I want to see you repeat the fence job. I'll be there."

Smith left with the note to Charlie; Joe Cross was told to return to his job and to get this particular gap well fenced before he quit that evening. I lined up Pinky, the wagon boss, and when Smith returned after delivering the note to Charlie, told them that the three of us would stand guard at the fenced water gap that night and meet Charlie when he rode in. I chose Smith because of his gunslinging reputation; Pinky as range foreman, of course, would be one to go. The water crossing fence which Charlie had torn down that morning was located where a dry wash went under a railroad bridge. Pinky, Smith and I arrived at the water gap about sundown; we tied our horses on the west side of the track and spent our time walking around within a few yards of the bridge. Time passed on—it was now about eleven at night, dark as pitch, with only a faint glow of light in the west.

Suddenly we could hear horses approaching, "There come the boys now," said Smith. We were all sitting down on top of the railroad grade. Immediately jumping to our feet, we tried to see into the dark, but one could have brought his hand up to his face without seeing it, so dark was the night. When we got up, Smith, Pinky, Murray and the bridge were to my left. I heard one of the boys to my left move and, turning my head, caught a glimpse of Smith between me and the dim light in the west, he was retreating under the bridge. In a moment I could hear Pinky following him. This so disgusted me that I crawled through the wires in the fence and started walking out alone to meet the men riding in. The horses immediately stampeded which told me it was only a bunch of range horses. I called to Smith and Pinky to come out—it was only a bunch of range mares.

I walked back to the railroad, making only one remark: "Well, boys, if this is the kind of fighting men I have with me we had better get back to the ranch." On the way home I would not talk to either of them. Smith tried to explain that it was the waiting that got him—if things came up quickly he was all right. Pinky, however, had no excuse to offer. Here was a gunslinger with a reputation, who ran from what he thought was going to be a fight. And apparently my note to Charlie, which called for a showdown, was all that was necessary, as his men never turned up.

I would like to tell you a little more about this gunslinger, his reputation, the two men he had killed, and how he came to be working for the Greene Cattle Company. Jay Smith, as I'm calling him, had killed two men that I had knowledge of; first, he killed one in Central City, New Mexico; second, and another in Temosachic, Chihuahua, Old Mexico.

The first victim of Smith was noted as a fighting man in his own right, but this time he was unarmed. Smith was tending bar in one of Central City's many saloons, for, like all western towns in the early 1900's, it was well dotted with saloons. A fellow came in for a drink or two, had Smith serve him one, then went over to one of the card tables, picked up a deck of cards and interested himself in a game of solitaire. Smith, noting that the visitor was unarmed, evidently started an argument; anyway the chap was shot down, and in the trial which followed, only Smith's story was in evidence. He claimed that his victim started abusing him and, jumping up from the table, started towards him with his fists raised, saying he intended to break every bone in Smith's body. Smith stepped from behind the bar with his six-shooter in his hand; said he warned his antagonist to stop or he would kill him. The man kept coming, Smith warned him again, but this time Smith shot him down. As there were no witnesses other than Smith, the deceased's reputation as a troublemaker was taken into consideration and Smith was cleared of the charge of murder. I have talked with men who were in Central City at the time and they called the killing plain murder.

In 1905 Smith showed up in Temosachic, where the Greene Gold and Silver Company had its headquarters. He spent most of his time in gambling. Smith's reputation preceded him and he was considered one of the West's noted gun slingers. It seems he had other notches on his gun. About this time a newcomer appeared in Temosachic and joined the gambling fraternity which was flocking to the new frontier in large droves. As the new man was also a gun slinger, having killed the town marshall in Douglas, Arizona, a few days before his arrival in Temosachic, everyone felt it was only a matter of time before these two were bound to clash.

Like most Mexican towns, Temosachic boasted of a plaza in the town center which was about two hundred feet square with some shrubbery and trees and a bandstand at its center. On opposite sides of the plaza were the only two saloons in town, owned and operated by Americans. Smith's headquarters were in one of these saloons and Mr. Newcomer's in the other. I do not know just what started the trouble between these two men although I was in Temosachic at the time, working for the Greene Gold and Silver Company. The quarrel had continued for several days. Smith had warned Newcomer to stay on his side of the Plaza and he had returned the warning. Old Man Diedrich and Sid Mullen, friends of both Smith and Newcomer, were trying to patch up the trouble between the two boys. They had talked Smith into agreeing to a truce provided they could get Baylor to do likewise.

They left Smith, crossed the Plaza to talk to the enemy, who, it seems, agreed to the truce; they returned to Smith and were lined up to the bar for a drink. The bar had a long mirror in back, and anyone facing the bar could see in the mirror anyone coming in the front door. Before they had time to tell Smith that Newcomer had agreed to a truce, he came crashing through the bat-wing doors. Smith, facing the mirror and recognizing Newcomer, immediately turned and started shooting; his first shot caught the man straight through his middle and into his spinal column. He fell to the floor and Smith, standing over him fired the balance of his shots at Newcomer but in his excitement missed him with all five shots. When Newcomer was picked up, his six-shooter was found under him, although both Diedrich and Mullen claimed that at no time did they see a gun in Newcomer's hand. Smith was arrested and served some time for this but was later pardoned on account of the testimony of Diedrich and Mullen that they had not had time to tell Smith that Baylor had agreed to a truce.

One day, about a year later, Jay Smith came riding in to the headquarters ranch of the Greene Cattle Company at Hereford, leading a pack horse loaded with his bedding, camp outfit and all. He presented me a note from the Cananea office to put him to work as a range detective. I drew a map of the range for Smith, gave him an order on the store for supplies needed, told him he was his own boss, and started him out. To this day I do not understand why Smith was unloaded on me—I really had no use for a range detective as conditions were rather clean on our ranges. I am under the impression that the Cananea outfit was afraid of him.

We had two of our men riding bog holes on the lower San Pedro pulling out any cattle which might get bogged down. The two boys, Jimmy Kane and Babe Glenn, were two fairly good ropers and, as the Fourth of July celebration in Bisbee was only a couple of weeks away, they asked permission of me to practice roping and tieing while riding bog. I gave my permission asking them to rope only young stock. Pinky, our wagon boss, was working over on the Babocomeri River so, in the absence of their chief, the boys had come to me for this permission.

Several days later, Pinky returned and was rounding up the Snake pasture to get a fresh supply of saddle horses for his outfit. We had a big round corral at the time on the west bank of the San Pedro just below the bridge where the highway now crosses the river. Fletcher, the store manager, poked his head in the office and advised that Pinky was just driving a bunch of horses into the corral. Leaving my gun and belt in the office, I untied my horse from the rack in front of the store and, mounting, rode over to the corral. I found Smith also at the corral; it seems he had noticed the boys rounding up the pasture and joined in with the work.

I was riding one of my top horses, a bay called Button. This horse had a wart about the size of a button in the middle of his chest, which accounts for his name. The boys were through separating the horses and two of them had been sent back to the Snake pasture with the horses not needed. Pinky and the rest of the boys were already mounted and on their way to the store—Smith was one of the last to leave. I had just mounted Button when I heard Babe Glenn tell Smith to "get down off that horse, you son of a b—." It seems that Pinky had told the boys that Smith had reported them for practicing roping while riding bog. Smith immediately pulled his gun, saying, "If you get off that horse I'll kill you." Here was another typical situation—Glenn was unarmed and Smith had a gun in his hand.

I was about seventy-five feet away, mounted but un-armed. I wrapped my quirt around Button's rear, intend-ing to ride up and pull Smith off his horse as I knew he would surely kill Glenn. "I'll kill you even if Axford is here." With this statement, he jumped off the left side of his horse and I heard him cock the gun as he piled off. I charged up on Button, jumped off and, rounding the rear of Smith's horse, came up behind him and, grabbing both his arms, said, "Don, put up your gun—this is no place to make a play of this kind." He was shaking all over but obeyed me and holstered his gun. Turning to Glenn, I told him, "Babe, you leave this fellow alone—he is too much for you."

We all rode over to the store; I went inside, strapped on my gun and went out to face Smith. I had given him a job of flagging out a road from Tombstone around a series of gullies above Lewis Springs on the lower river; the county commissioners had promised to improve this road if I would work out the route. I called Smith over to one side and, dropping down using my finger in the dust, marked out the proposed road above the Lewis Springs gullies and asked Smith if he had properly marked the crossing at this point. He said he had tied rags on mes-quite bushes on each side of the wash. I then told him that I was through with him and for him to report back to Cananea. You may wonder here just why Smith did not attempt to kill me. The story told about Smith quit-ting me at the bridge may explain this.

Smith would fight when scared, would shoot a man down rather than engage in a fist fight, also would kill you if he knew he was faster on the draw; he was what I call a very dangerous man. He often tried to get me to draw and shoot at a bottle alongside the trail or road. I understood Smith; as long as I was unknown, my speed on the draw, etc. he would be afraid to go against me. I always answered him that I never pulled a gun unless I intended to use it. He once kidded me about my old scabbard, said I might get hurt unless I got a better one. My answer to that was that it was the fastest scabbard I had ever used and I intended to keep it. All this confused Smith or he would have jumped me when I fired him before the whole outfit.

A New House at the Ranch

The old headquarters residence had been destroyed by fire and the company was building a new house for Moson. We had an old codger named Steve Wilson getting out some marble blocks from a ledge up in the Huachucas to be used in the foundation and the pillar bases on the porch which surrounded the house on three sides. Steve had not been on the job long before he was labeled with a nickname which stayed with him for years. He had sent down a note to me asking for a couple of Mexican miners; I hired two who both said they were good hammer men. The following day both returned to be paid off for one day's work, and with them a note from Steve, saying, "Axford, these men are not miners; neither one could hit a bull in the hind end with a banjo." From then on he was called "Banjo Steve."

In due time the new headquarters residence was completed and the boss moved in with his family. A colored couple had been hired, the man to take care of the newly planted yard and to look after the family team of carriage horses; the woman to do the cooking. On the sideboard was kept a glass decanter of whiskey which was replenished from time to time from the supply on hand at the company store. As the outfit was one of the large cattle spreads on the Mexican border and as cattle were constantly being taken across the line from Mexico to Arizona, it often was necessary to have government officials as guests, as duty had to be paid and cattle inspected for fever ticks in order to protect the Arizona ranges. This will, I hope, explain the need for the whiskey decanter on the sideboard.

Anyway, one day the railroad set in on the sidetrack. The home ranch being located on the railroad, a carload of office furniture and supplies arrived from the old man's New York office which he had closed in order to devote more time to his vast interests in Arizona and Old Mexico. The only place where this could be protected and stored successfully was in the attic of the new headquarters residence, as the furnishings consisted of several fine rugs, among them a couple of mountain lion rugs with the heads mounted thereon, and an enormous bear rug. When moving the furniture to the attic we found a small barrel about half full of whiskey which, from the burnt-in figures on the barrel, showed that its contents were thirty-five years old.

Several months passed and one day the boss suggested that, as the old man would never call for the small barrel of whiskey, we tap the barrel and use it for the sideboard instead of the bar whiskey. It was about time for the fall term to start in our little school and some kind of arrangements had to be made to board and room the new teacher who was to arrive in a day or two. The boss's Missus agreed that the teacher could lodge with her. When the teacher arrived she was found to be about twenty-two years of age and very pretty and so innocent and nice that all off-color stories were tabooed in her presence, and if one of us accidentally bumped into her when passing in the hall, apologies were immediately in order.

I had just returned from an inspection trip from the other side of the range when I met the boss over at the store; almost the first question he asked me was if I had been hitting the decanter more than usual of late. I told Frank that I had not taken any kind of a drink for a week or two, that I was having some trouble with my stomach and was off all drinks until it was cleared up. "Somebody is sure working on it and no doubt it's that darkie. As long as it was bar whiskey," said Frank, "I did not pay too much attention, but I'll be damned if we are going to furnish Sambo with thirty-five-year-old stuff. I am going to Bisbee tomorrow and I am going to set up a trap for him." Well, the boss went to Bisbee, got a quart of regular whiskey and took it to a druggist and asked him how much croton oil he could safely put in the whiskey, explaining about Sambo and his desire to teach him a lesson. The druggist said he would fix up the whiskey himself as it would be dangerous if mixed by someone who did not know what he was doing. Frank returned to the ranch and he and I went over, took out the precious stuff and filled the decanter with the croton oil mixture.

The next morning the boss, upon getting up, went out to the kitchen as usual to say good morning to Mandy, the cook, and asked her how she was. "I'se alright, Mr. Frank, but that ole man of mine he's powerful sick—he took the back-door trots about ten o'clock last night and has been goin' ever since, and the funny thing, Mr. Frank, the school teacher is right along with him." The teacher lost about fifteen pounds off her weight, the kids had an unexpected vacation and at the end of the month she moved to another boarding house. While we never said a word about this, ever afterward, when meetng the school teacher, she seemed to have a question mark in her eyes. We felt sure we were going to trap Sambo—but the teacher was quite a surprise.

Moson had placed a man and wife at Lewis Springs at the lower end of our land, with the hopes that they would be able to make some kind of a picnic resort out of it; they proved to be not capable of handling the job and we wanted to replace them, in order to give someone else a chance. To do this, it was necessary to buy some chickens and stock which they had on the place. The man had run off and left his wife to face things; I rode down to see her and made arrangements to buy her out. However, she would not accept a check so it was necessary for me to go to Bisbee to get the money.

I had to stay overnight in Bisbee and while there I had two men pointed out to me and was told the following story of their marriages which, I was given to understand, had proved very successful. One was Shorty and the other, Ben. They were inseparable companions, both were bachelors and had no use for women, and were part owners of several mining claims lying at the south end of the Mule Mountains just to the west of Lowell. Shorty was a hardrock miner and Ben belonged to the gambling fraternity which at the time was to be found in and around the many mining camps in Arizona. They batched together in a small shack on the outskirts of Lowell.

One of the pardners in the mining claims received in his mail one morning a "Heart and Hand" letter from some association located in St. Louis, Missouri, enclosing a group of pictures of prospective brides seeking husbands. Among these were pictures of two sisters of Swedish descent which showed them as being above the average in good looks. He passed the letter and pictures over to a group of men and, in the discussion which the letter provoked, one man told of a friend of his up in Colorado who had married one of the "Heart and Hand" girls and found her to be all one could ask for as a wife and companion.

As the group was discussing the pros and cons of this method of finding a wife, Shorty and Ben came in, passed by the group with the usual wave of the hand and bellied up to the bar for their morning drink. Everyone in the group had often heard Shorty and Ben express their dislike for all women and one of the boys suggested giving the letter and pictures to the pair. "Let's do better than that," suggested one of the mining claim pardners; "let's write to a couple of the girls, have a couple of us sign the letters, but get pictures of Shorty and Ben to be enclosed in the letter; in this way we can have a lot of fun." It was thought by the group that the two Swede sisters were the ones to whom to write. A letter was composed and forwarded to the two girls; they could not find pictures of Shorty and Ben to enclose in the first letter, but signing it, it was stamped and sent on its way.

In due time an answer arrived and the sisters were very much interested, stating that they had always wanted to come west and to be married to western men; they also wanted pictures to be sent in the next letter. The boys finally managed to get a picture of Shorty and Ben, which was sent on to the sisters. By this time half of the town was in on the fun. The reply from the sisters was prompt and to the point; both agreed to marry Ben and Shorty and also to come to Lowell, providing transportation was sent. This caused a little more excitement than expected among the group. One suggested that they write the girls, calling off the whole thing. At this point one of the mining pardners spoke up. "No," he said, "let's go through with it. Send transportation, arrange somehow to have Shorty and Ben meet the train, and if they refuse to go through with the deal, the girls can easily find work in Bisbee or Lowell, and, as women are scarce here, will no doubt find several other good men in the camp, who would be willing to marry the girls."

Transportation was arranged through the railroad agent, with instructions that they be notified of the exact time of arrival in Lowell. This was necessary in order to have Shorty and Ben meet the train. This caused considerable discussion of just how this could be brought about without arousing the suspicion of the two. They got hold of some letterheads of one of the local mining companies, had a letter written thereon, stating that the company was interested in their claims and wanted one of their engineers to look over the mines. This letter was shown Shorty and Ben and it was agreed to accept the offer, and that they would make arrangements to meet the train and transport the engineer to the claims. As the two girls and Shorty and Ben would make a party of four, it was necessary to arrange for a two-seated surrey to meet the train. Shorty and Ben were real excited over the possibility of selling the claims; they had been doing assessment work on them for several years and were anxious to see some returns come in.

The great day finally arrived, the railroad agent notified the boys that the girls would arrive at seven-thirty that evening. Another letter was written on company letterhead advising Shorty and Ben and his pardners that two mining engineers would arrive that evening on the seven-thirty train and to arrange to meet them as agreed. By this time most of the town had been alerted and by seven o'clock various groups could be seen slowly walking towards the station which was about a half mile to the west of the town. It had been agreed Shorty and Ben were to meet the engineers and bring them to the hotel for a meeting with all the pardners. The train was a little late, and dusk had commenced to settle over the valley by the time it finally pulled in. The lateness of the hour had enabled about fifty of Lowell's citizens, including several women, to get close to the station without being observed by Shorty and Ben. The two had tied their team a short distance away and were on the station platform when the train pulled in. The two sisters were the only persons to get off the train, spotted Shorty and Ben, and rushed up, trying to embrace them. This brought prompt reaction—the two men backed away with the statement, "What's the matter with you girls—are you crazy?" "Why you sent for us, didn't you?" "I should say not," said Ben. By this time the four were almost surrounded by the group who had walked out to see the fun.

"What goes on here" asked a big six-foot miner. The girls explained that Shorty and Ben had sent them transportation and were now trying to get out of their agreement, stating that they had been corresponding with the boys for some time. The men claimed this was a damn lie, that they had never written any letters. "What proof have you girls? These men are well-known citizens and unless you have proof there is nothing we can do about it." The girls then produced the pictures of Shorty and Ben, which completely changed the situation. The two looked at the pictures with bewildered expressions but admitted that the picture was of them. By this time the crowd started to get mad; asked Shorty and Ben just what they intended to do. "You had better make up your minds fast; we are rather disgusted with the dirty way you are treating these girls." The boys had had plenty of time to observe the two sisters and admired the way they had conducted themselves. Ben made his decision first, and turning to Shorty, he asked, "Shorty, are you game?" (Shorty agreed he was willing and, reaching for the luggage of the sisters, they were on their way to the buggy.) A cheer went up from the crowd and the group surrounding the buggy went off singing down the hill. Ben and Shorty married the Swedish girls and Lowell had one of its greatest celebrations, and an Arizona celebration is something to write home about.

Often my work called me to Naco when we were passing cattle from Mexico into Arizona and many a time I had the pleasure of meeting B. J. O'Reilly. This gentleman was manager and part owner of the Naco Townsite Company. The little town of Naco was located on the international boundary line between the United States and Mexico about nine miles south of Bisbee where the Phelps Dodge Company had its famous Copper Queen Mine. This mine had been developed to a point where large bodies of ore which had been uncovered, coupled with the production from the Pilares mine in Nacozari, Sonora, called for the building of a large smelter to take care of the immense tonnage developed. In order to take care of the extensive plans, suitable flat grounds had to be found upon which to build the large smelter which would be required.

The little town of Naco was in the midst of such flat land and had the additional advantage of already being the terminal of the freight haul for supplies in and out from the mining operations in Nacozari and where the railroad between Benson and Bisbee, which was also owned by the Phelps Dodge people, had a spur from which the Nacozari supplies were taken care of. The Phelps Dodge Company had been trying to get a better freight rate from the Southern Pacific Company on its tonnage of copper mat which in those days had to be shipped east for further refining. The railroad company had refused the mining company the rates wanted, resulting in connections being made with the El Paso and Southwestern, a new railroad group who agreed to build west from El Paso to Bisbee. Grading work was also to be started from the Bisbee end. It was the intention of the Phelps Dodge people to run a railroad south from their spur in Naco to their holdings in Nacozari, thereby bringing the concentrates from Nacozari to the smelter which was planned for Naco. This would give them a downgrade haul from Bisbee and do away with the long haul from Nacozari which was now being performed by freight teams.

B. J. O'Reilly, being a smart operator, had tuned in on the gossip about the big operations planned and had been expecting a visit from company officials. He was not kept waiting long. A committee did call, discussed the plans to run a line south to Nacozari from Naco, and pointed out to O'Reilly that he could expect a town of a few thousand people instead of the one hundred and fifty inhabitants which the town boasted. What the committee wanted from the Naco Townsite people was a gift of land, enough to take care of the railroad yards and warehouses which would be necessary to handle their operations. O'Reilly listened to the plans and the request. Firmly believing that, as already Naco was being used as a terminal for Nacozari supplies and as the railroad spur was already there, he had the company where they would have to agree to his terms, he answered their request for a gift of land with this statement. "Gentlemen, the Naco Townsite Company had land to sell—none to give away." The meeting broke up, the committee returned to Bisbee badly disappointed with O'Reilly's answer.

The western end of the grading for the railroad from El Paso to Bisbee was started from Don Louis station and O'Reilly could easily see the grade as it advanced along the hills south and east of Bisbee. The committee, believing that O'Reilly, after thinking things over, would realize his mistake and listen to common sense reasoning, again approached him for a better answer. While O'Reilly could plainly see the grading along the hills he was convinced that the Nacozari line could only be extended from the spur in Naco. He smiled when he saw the committee approaching his office and wasted no time in advising them that his position was the same, but with this exception, that the price of the land had advanced. That night, out of Bisbee rushed Charlie Overlock, Alfred Paul and one or two others, and a townsite was located on the international line at a point in the center of Sulphur Springs Valley. This town was named Douglas, in honor of James Douglas who was the manager of the Bisbee operations for the Phelps Dodge Company. The railroad was built from El Paso to Bisbee, the line extended south to Nacozari, Sonora, and today Douglas is a prosperous city of twenty-five or thirty thousand people, while Naco has about the same one hundred and fifty inhabitants it had when B. J. O'Reilly owned the town.

It pays sometimes not to be too sure. O'Reilly never lived down his boner and for years was often asked, "What's the price of Naco lots today, O'Reilly?"

I had to make a business trip to Las Cruces, New Mexico and as it was necessary to remain several days before completing my business, I got very well acquainted with several local citizens and was filled in on the story of Oliver Lee as the one man who had out-fought Pat Garrett, the killer of the famous Billy the Kid. Las Cruces was a divided city—about 80 percent of its people favored Oliver and felt he was being unjustly persecuted.

Old Man Fountain and his son had disappeared. His buckboard and team had been found on the edge of the white sands which cover a part of Dōna Ana County in New Mexico. Fountain had left Las Cruces on his way to Lincoln County, supposedly on his way to prosecute certain charges against Oliver Lee and Jim Gilliland, cattle ranchers. For some reason Lee had incurred the enmity of the political bosses of New Mexico and as people were told that Fountain, who was a lawyer, was on his way to Lincoln County at the time of his disappearance to prosecute Lee for whatever cause, public sentiment was easily swayed to point the finger of suspicion at Lee, with respect to Fountain's disappearance.

A couple or three years passed, and every year the group after Lee tried to get a grand jury to indict him. Grand juries refused for it could not be proved that Fountain was dead—neither the body of Fountain nor his son had been found. It was necessary, if Lee was ever to be indicted, to arrange for a jury that would bring in an indictment and also to have a sheriff who would be willing to go after Lee, who happened to be a man who feared no man, and also a respected citizen. This brought Pat Garrett, the famous killer of Billy the Kid, into the picture. Garrett had been brought in against Billy the Kid in what was more or less a political war, and was for hire. Garrett was installed as sheriff and a grand jury found to bring in the sought-after indictment. Dõna Ana County was evenly divided about this—many believed Lee to be innocent, and he had many friends in Las Cruces who kept him advised of any movements made by Garrett. So when Garrett was getting a posse together to serve the warrant on Lee, riders immediately left Las Cruces to advise him that Garrett and his men would soon be on their way. Lee, knowing he was innocent and that it was a political battle, knew if he gave up he would in all probability be killed, so he and Gilliland made up their minds to fight it out and under no circumstances to submit to arrest by Garrett.

Lee's ranch house was an adobe structure with what is known as a fire wall around the top edge of the flat roof, with pipe outlets at certain intervals to drain the water from the roof. This fire wall was about two feet above the roof top and extended all the way around the top of the house. A rider from Las Cruces had ridden in ahead of the posse and advised Lee and Gilliland that Garrett was on the way. The boys moved some bedding up on the roof, with some water and provisions, intending to make their fight from behind the fire wall, which would provide very good protection. They had figured that Garrett and his men would slip up close under cover of the night and make their attack under the protection of some outbuildings which were located about fifty or sixty yards from the house. The outhouses consisted of a small shed used as a stable and a windmill tower which was enclosed around the bottom making a room which was used to house tools and the like.

True to form, Garrett opened up on the house just at daylight, fired several shots through the doors and windows, calling for Lee and Gilliland to come out with their hands up. They grabbed their Winchesters and using the fire wall for protection easily kept Garrett and the posse behind the outbuildings. Finally, after several minutes of fighting, one of Garrett's men, a little braver than the rest, started a run towards the house. This man was immediately dropped by Lee and fell in the yard a few feet from the house. By this time the sun was up—the man shot down in the yard was calling for help. Several minutes passed, the wounded man kept calling for someone to come and help him. Lee, unable to stand the man's pleadings, called to Garrett and asked him what he intended to do, if he was going to leave the man or was he going to help him. "At least get him out of the way," was his comment. Garrett said they were willing to try to help the man if Lee would agree not to shoot while this was being done. Lee told Garrett to come ahead, "But remember, you are coming up under cover of our guns, so don't start anything." The posse came out and, looking the wounded man over, decided he needed a doctor, so the entire posse, Garrett and all, left to get a doctor. As soon as they had left, Lee and Gilliland came down off the house, moved the wounded man inside and tried to make him comfortable. Lee, in questioning the wounded man, found that a reward of five thousand dollars had been offered for him dead or alive and that each member of the posse was being paid five dollars per day. They saw the man was badly wounded and would die. Lee immediately left to get a notary public to take down the dying man's statements. This was done. Garrett and the doctor never returned.

Several months later, Lee agreed to give up, provided he would not have to surrender his sidearms. Arrangements were made, Lee was placed in the custody of a United States marshal and removed to El Paso, Texas, while waiting for trial. A. B. Fall was engaged by Lee and

Gilliland to defend them against the charge of murder. Fall got a change of venue and the case came to trial in Socorro. On the opening day of the trial, many of Lee's friends rode into Socorro and quickly established their headquarters on one side of the main street, Garrett and his men on the opposite side. The feeling was so strong against Garrett and his political group that had a fire-cracker been set off in the street, a battle would have been fought that would have made the Lincoln County War look like child's play. Luckily no battle was fought.

Lee was easily cleared of the charge. In fact, as soon as the dying man's deposition was introduced, the prosecution stopped its proceedings and exerted all its power to defend the politician responsible for getting a jury to indict without sufficient evidence and the bringing in of Pat Garrett to serve the warrant. It was also proven at the trial that there was no case against Lee in the Lincoln County court at the time of Fountain's disappearance. This did away with any motive which could connect Lee with the crime, if a crime was committed.

To this day the disappearance of Fountain and his boy is one of the great mysteries of the West. Some claim that he had been seen several times in Old Mexico; this, however, was never proved. It is known, however, that Garrett, after the fight at Lee's ranch, had a wholesome respect for the fighting ability of Oliver Lee and went out of his way to avoid him.

Billy the Kid standing in the open door with the moonlight behind him was an easy victim for the sheriff but Oliver Lee and Gilliland ready and willing to fight it out were a different story.

The Santa Cruz Reservoir
and Land Company

Mr. Greene had started a new company, to be known as the Santa Cruz Reservoir and Land Company with head offices in Tucson. It was to be engaged in clearing desert lands and building a diversion dam to turn the floodwaters of the Santa Cruz River into a reservoir, also to be built; from this reservoir were to spread canals and ditches to irrigate the thousands of acres of land which were to be brought under cultivation.

I had been asked to join Mr. Greene when his private car the "Verde" passed through Hereford, as he wished to talk with me about representing him on a ranch which he intended to buy in Texas. I joined Mr. Greene and he told me he was on a deal to purchase the Goodnight Ranch and he was going to send me down to look after his interests if the deal went through. Greene was on his way to Toltec, a station on the Southern Pacific Railroad about 66 miles west of Tucson. Vic Griffith, one of the men interested with Mr. Greene in the Santa Cruz project, was to join him at Tucson and go with him to Toltec. Mr. Greene asked me to stay on the "Verde" and make the trip with him. At Toltec we were met by a Mr. Forbes, the superintendent in charge of the work and we spent most of the day going over the desert land which he was busy clearing of brush and mesquite roots. Forbes had established his camp about three miles south of the railroad where he had his commissary and cook tents put up, and one or two tents for the Mexican laborers. The runoff of floodwaters of the Santa Cruz River water shed had been carefully checked for several years back and the project looked feasible.

I had just returned to Hereford when I received a telegram from Mr. Greene asking me to return to Tucson and report to Mr. Manning and Vic Griffith. It seems that these two men had been having some trouble with Mr. Forbes; he had gone into Tucson and had cussed them out and they were afraid for some reason to fire him and had asked Mr. Greene to send someone over to take charge. I understood that the deal for the Goodnight Ranch had fallen through and I was to take charge at Toltec. I reported to Manning and Griffith who were very glad to see me, and advised me to expect trouble with Forbes when I got to Toltec; however I had no difficulty relieving Mr. Forbes, who left at once for Tucson. I never did learn what the trouble was with Forbes.

Greene got behind the project with his usual energy; ordered three Kennard-Haines gasoline tractors and a J. I.

Case steam tractor. We bolted heavy railroad rails together and were soon busy clearing the desert lands of all
brush and wood. We burned the brush but kept the
mesquite roots in piles to be used as fuel for the camps. A
Mr. Scott was hired with 30 teams, scrapers, ploughs,
etc., to build the reservoir dam at the location chosen by
the engineers. A Major Wright had two crews of surveyors
running out contour lines and surveying the canals and
laterals. Soon we had four separate camps running, put
down wells at the different camps and found the water
level at 85 feet. Our biggest problem was keeping
cooks—I had cooks on the job, cooks leaving and cooks
coming. I finally solved the problem by keeping a couple
extra cooks working with the clearing gang as helpers on
the tractors, ready to step in the moment a cook went
haywire.

As I was working very close to Mr. Greene and usually
stayed on his private car whenever he was on the desert, I
got to hear several interesting stories. One about his
meeting with Geronimo, the famous Apache Chief,
follows: Bill Greene and his pardner Jim Kirk were
driving along a road in Sonora, Mexico, just a few miles
south of the international boundary. The outfit consisted
of a team of horses hitched to a light wagon which was
carrying their camp outfit, bedding, personal belongings
and a supply of grub.

They were driving in open flat country and were approaching a small range of hills when fired upon by
Indians and one of the horses shot down. The Indians
were in the rocks about halfway up one of the hills which
curved in from the flat plain. Inside the curve of the hills
was a cluster of rocks jutting up from the floor of the
plain and about eighty yards from the hill and fifty yards
from the road on which they were riding. Greene and

Kirk, grabbing their Winchesters, saw at a glance that the only fighting chance they had was to make a run and gain the protection of this small clump of rocks. To do so, they had to run towards the Indians who were pouring in a heavy fire on the wagon. Fortunately they made the shelter of the rocks and were surprised that the Indians immediately stopped their fire and evidently pulled out at once without attempting to take advantage of the situation. Greene said they might have got an Indian or two before being killed themselves, but that would have been all, for the rocks gave very poor protection.

Several months after this one-sided battle, Geronimo was captured by United States soldiers and he and his band taken to La Morita, a small port of entry on the Mexican border. Greene happened to be in La Morita when Geronimo and his band were brought in, and as Greene talked fluent Spanish, he engaged the old chief in conversation, telling Geronimo that he was one of the two men in the fight in the plain and said he had been bothered ever since by the thought of the Indians suddenly stopping the battle and pulling out. "You had us where we could not have got away; why did you stop shooting?" Geronimo said, "You were too brave to be killed so I called off the Indians. You ran straight towards us, proving you were courageous men."

Greene had always been thankful after this experience that the rocks were in the position they were; had he and Jim had to run the other direction away from the Indians to get to the protection of the rocks, it would have had a different ending. What appeared to Geronimo to be bravery was an attempt by Kirk and Greene to take advantage of the only shelter offered on the level plain.

Greene also told of the ore body the Guggenheims missed. For several years the famous mining family, the

Guggenheim brothers, had been doing development work on the Pilares group of claims a few miles out from Nacozari, Mexico. During these years about one thousand feet of tunnels, shafts, and raises had been driven in an attempt to find a body of ore large enough to justify a smelter or concentration plant which would be necessary to make any mine furnish the dividends required. As the property was at that time about eight miles south of the Mexican border, all concentrations or smelter mats would have to be hauled by freight teams this great distance in order to reach the railroad at Naco.

It is true that Pilares on the surface had made quite a showing of good ore but the thousand feet of tunnels and shafts had not proven to the Guggenheims that there was a body of ore large enough to justify any more expenditure of money. As far as they were concerned, the Pilares would never make a mine. It is proper, I believe, to state at this point in our story that the Guggenheim brothers and associates were ranked with the world's greatest mining experts.

In trying to salvage something from the operations, the Pilares mine was offered to anyone for fifty percent of the machinery and supplies now on the property. The Phelps Dodge Corporation had kept tab on the Pilares operations and, while the company was not interested in taking over the mine after the famous Guggenheims had turned it down, the subject did come up before their board of directors in one of its meetings. The Phelps Dodge people had a geologist working for them, known as Dr. L. D. Ricketts. Doc appeared before the Board and begged the company to buy the Pilares, stating he would stake his reputation on making it a paying mine. Now the company thought a great deal of Dr. Ricketts' judgment and, as there was not a great deal of money involved, finally agreed to purchase the property. The Board called Doc in and advised him of their decision, stating that while they felt they were throwing away money, they would take the chance and would send him down in charge of the operations, to make good on his statements and to try to save his reputation.

The rest of the story is mining history. Dr. Ricketts took over the Pilares mine and in a few months developed an enormous body of ore; a diamond drill was used to determine the depth, width, and length of this immense body of ore; a large concentrate plant was built and the railroad extended from Douglas to Nacozari. The verdict on the Pilares is that it will be a producing mine when Bisbee is forgotten.

I also heard Mr. Greene tell several times of his meeting with E. H. Harriman. It may be said that Colonel William Cornell Greene in his earlier days had tried in several different ways to make his fortune and had promoted one or two mining ventures which, however, had failed to make the grade. But Greene kept trying and at last had got hold of copper property that, with its mineral showing coupled with a good price for copper, looked promising enough to start looking for capital.

With this thought in mind, after borrowing enough money for the trip from his old friend, B. A. Packard, Greene headed for New York City which, in that time as now, was the financial capital of the world. Here the great financial wizards of the day made their headquarters. Greene arrived in New York, took quarters at the Waldorf and started his quest. The time was right, the price of copper twenty-five cents, and also Henry H. Rogers was in the process of putting together his dream of Amalgamated Copper. Rogers and his associates had bought the Marcus Daly holdings in Butte, Montana, had it recapitalized, the company increasing to seventy million, placed the stock on the market where it was immediately gobbled up by the buying public. Through this financial wizardry, after the stock issue had been sold, it was said at the time that the Butte holdings were clear velvet to Rogers and associates.

Greene was a real promoter; he lost no time in contacting the Rogers group, produced his ore samples and his property papers and some part of this group got behind Greene, and the Cobra Grande Copper Company of Cananea, Sonora, Mexico was launched in great style.

Some months later the great stock manipulator, Tom Lawson, started his famous series of Frenzied Finance which was published in *Everybody's Magazine*. In this series he took occasion to make several unkind remarks about different mining companies and in one issue took a slap at the Cobre Grande Copper Company. This caused a wave of selling on curb and exchange and Greene found he was compelled to buy back his stock in order to support the price or go under. He had to have sufficient capital to do this—and quick. In rustling around for help he was advised to see E. H. Harriman who at that time was heavily invested in the railroad world and also one of New York's smartest stock manipulators. Greene had never met Harriman but, working fast, made an appointment to meet Harriman the next day at two o'clock.

Greene's first intention was to ask Harriman for five hundred thousand dollars; when he stepped out of his cab at the curb, he mentally made it a million; when he stepped out of the elevator on the second floor where Harriman had his office, he upped the price in his mind to two million. Greene was ushered in to meet Harriman, they talked of the West and things in general before getting down to the business at hand. Finally Harriman broke the ice by asking Greene what he could do for him. Greene explained the situation, stating he would need financial help to protect his mining stock on the market. "How much money will you need?" asked Harriman. "Two million dollars," said Greene. At this moment Harriman paused and seemed to be thinking things over. Greene momentarily thought all is lost—he is going to refuse the loan. Then Harriman, looking Greene straight in the eye, made these comments in his reply. "I have watched your career in the market, Greene, and the fact that you have asked for two million dollars proves to me that you understand the market, so I am going to let you have the money. But if you had asked for a cent less I would not have given it to you. It will take two million to carry you through."

The Cobre Grande Copper Company afterwards became the famous Greene Cananea Copper Company which produced its millions for its stockholders. I had often heard Greene tell this story, winding up with the statement that the good Lord must have been looking after him, or why did he ask for two million when in his ignorance he had thought that five hundred thousand would have been more than enough. It took the two million dollars to save what was then the Cobre Grande Copper Company.

And then there was the story of a F. Augustus Heinze of Butte, Montana, and how he took advantage of the Apex Law. This law was in force in the earlier days in several western states and allowed anyone who could prove that the vein or lode of ore apexed on their ground could follow the ore across adjoining claims right into the other's territory. At the time of this story the state of Montana had such a law.

Working for one of the Anaconda Mining Companies

was a mining engineer named F. Augustus Heinze. In surveying out the different claims which crisscrossed on the famous Anaconda hill, he found a triangular piece of ground which was open for filing on. This Anaconda hill ranked as one of the richest bodies of ore in the world, another Comstock lode, so to speak, and was owned by the group which had bought out the Marcus Daly interests and was in the process of forming the Amalgamated Copper Company then under the control of H. H. Rogers and associates. Heinze immediately filed a claim on this triangle and started sinking a shaft. In some way he got control of the state politically, elected his own group to office and by proving in court that the ore on the hill apexed on his claim, got an injunction against the Anaconda Companies, stopping them entirely from mining. Heinze then rushed the work on his shaft, drifted over from the shaft on all sides and started to take out the ores that rightfully belonged to the Rogers group. H. H. Rogers was furious but helpless; for once he was completely whipped and by an upstart, F. Augustus Heinze.

It was quickly seen that the only way to get Heinze off their backs was to buy him out. At one time Heinze had agreed on the price and the closing meeting was arranged. Heinze walked into this meeting with a piece of paper in his hands which he told Rogers he must sign before the deal could be completed. This paper called for Rogers to sign a statement that for once the mighty system which he represented had been beaten at their own game. Rogers was furious and refused to sign and the meeting broke up. Finally some kind of a deal was made and Heinze sold out to the Rogers interests. Thenceforth, in a number of mining districts, regulations were established to invalidate the Apex Law.

F. Augustus Heinze took his gains from Montana and, joining with a man named Morse who was known as the Ice King of New York, bought control of two or three banks and started to play the stock market. About this time Tom Lawson was hired to write his famous story, "Frenzied Finance." In showing how stocks were manipulated in those days, in one of his chapters, Lawson mentioned F. Augustus Heinze and made a prophecy that the system "will get you, Heinze," for its arm is long and powerful. Heinze was out on a limb with his banks, for he evidently had been using some of the funds to play the market, and was vulnerable. A great number of you will remember the 1907 ninety-day panic, when we had to use scrip instead of cash. In some manner a shortage of cash was created and caused a run on the Heinze and Morse banks, which broke them. Morse was convicted and sent to the penitentiary at Atlanta, where he was later pardoned by President Taft. Lawson's prophecy proved out—the arm of vengeance was long and powerful.

* * *

It was at Toltec that I first met Ed Massey. Massey, like Jim Kirk, was one of Greene's early day cronies and helped in the development of the Cobre Grande Copper Company which later became the famous Greene Cananea Copper Company. Ed Massey, who used to be a government soldier, once located at Fort Apache, told about the famous horse race between the Apaches and the Navajos. The Apaches had been quietly living on the reservation for several years. Now and then a young buck, one usually with a college education, kicked over the traces and took to the trail, but usually did not stay out over a few months before he returned to the reservation of his own accord, settling down into the peaceful routine of rations issued by Uncle Sam and nothing to do but play. It was logical under the circumstances that the excitement, so necessary to the restless soul, must find expression in some manner, so the bucks took to gambling, foot races and horse racing. In fact, any form of game was interesting, providing it was a game of chance.

Fort Apache was the headquarters for the United States troops. Here, naturally was the playground for Indian and soldier alike. Here many a monte game lasted the long night through and many a horse race enlivened the monotonous life of native and soldier. As Ed Massey told the story at the time, about two hundred and fifty troopers and civilians made up the post personnel. None of them, except the packers and teamsters, had been in sight of a town of any kind for several months. As Uncle Sam's paydays came around in regular time, the accumulation of funds among the soldiers had commenced to hurt. They played monte and poker until the attraction had died out and were in the market for any game that would create excitement.

One of the soldiers owned a race horse which had won every race it had entered. The Apaches had been cleaned up so many times by "Old Bay" that it was impossible to get them interested in running against him. On the contrary, there were but few Indians on the reservation who would not bet their wigwam on Old Bay any time, any place, against any horse in the world. About this time notice was received through government channels that the Navajo tribe to the north had received permission to pay a friendly visit to the Apache Reservation for the purpose of barter and exchange. The Navajos were sending down about fifty Indians with ponies and homemade articles. The Apache was told to get his trading clothes on, with a view to stocking up with blankets and rugs, which the Navajo tribe was noted for making.

In due time the Navajos arrived. In addition to a

remuda of about two hundred ponies, they were well stocked with such articles of trade as buckskin gloves, rugs, blankets, and dried meat or jerky. They were in charge of an old chief, who announced upon arrival that their stay would be for ten days. Immediately the buying and bartering commenced. The Navajo would trade for anything he could use, and many an Apache horse and cow found its way into the Navajo herd. As the government furnished blankets, food, and clothing to the soldiers, most of the trading was done with the Indians, and from day to day the soldiers saw the Navajos getting richer and richer as the sale and exchange went on. One night in the barracks, after a discussion of things in general, one of the soldiers conceived the bright idea of trying to get a horse race out of the Navajos to win back some of these riches with Old Bay.

A committee was appointed to feel out the old Navajo chief, with instructions to go the limit as to the amount to bet. When they broached the matter to the old chief he seemed indifferent, said he did not have a race horse with him, that the fame of Old Bay was known to the Navajos and they did not think they had any business trying to beat him. All would have been well, if this committee had remained sober. But getting hold of some liquor, they proceeded to drink and made another trip over to see the old chief. They rode the old man unmercifully, called him a coward and finally shaking some three hundred dollars in currency under his nose, offered to run Old Bay against anything in his remuda. The chief, under coaching from one of his educated bucks, finally agreed to run, had his young buck draw up an agreement in writing to the effect that the committee would run against any horse in his remuda, covered the three hundred dollars, and the race was on.

They agreed to run on the last day of the Navajos'

visit. This gave them six days to train and to get Old Bay ready. The old chief asked and received permission to use one of the stalls to keep his horse in, and was granted the use of the post track to train on. The following morning two Navajo bucks arrived at the stable leading a blaze-faced, stocking-legged sorrel, weighing around nine hundred, and as pretty as a picture. For two days the boys tried to get a line on this sorrel, but it was impossible to find the horse alone. Always the two bucks were present, and they would only train him when the track was clear. The boys conceived the idea of stealing the sorrel out to try him with Old Bay, but never could get by the two Indians constantly on guard. A bottle of Old Crow did the trick. With both Indians laid out and dead to the world, they slipped the sorrel out and, under the bright Arizona moon, Old Bay beat him easily. They made a second race of it to be sure. No doubt of it, Old Bay was too fast for the Indian horse. That night every soldier and civilian collected everything of value. The next day saw some of the wildest betting the border had ever witnessed, with the Navajos covering every bet offered. When they ran out of money they put up the blankets, ponies, and saddles. The Apaches were slipped the good news and joined in. Numerous ponies, cows, and steers were driven to the corral where all stakes were gathered.

The day of the race was beautiful. By race time, 2:00 P. M., the crowd had gathered. Friendly slaps were exchanged by soldiers and Apaches alike and, under the tonic effect of a sure thing, happiness was prevailing. A few belated bets were laid. The sorrel was being led back and forth at the head of the track. Old Bay had been trotted sharply through and back in the warming up process. The old chief rode up, held up his hand for silence and, producing the signed agreement, had it read by one of his young bucks. "You have agreed to run against any horse in my remuda," said he. "I am going to run this red roan, instead of the sorrel." The boys held up the race until they discussed the situation with the commander of the post. They were told there was nothing to be done but to go through with the race. "You have made this bet in good faith. Our honor is involved, so make the best of it. Maybe Old Bay can pull you out."

A friendly curtain is drawn over the finish. There is an old saying that a soldier broke is a good soldier. Fort Apache had, for several months, some of the best soldiers in the service.

I Take a Vacation and
Head for the Northwest

For two years southern Arizona had had a serious drought; the Santa Cruz River had very little runoff, resulting in only a small amount of water finding its way into the reservoir. The surveying crew under Major Wright had run out a line from a point on the Gila River which showed it was feasible to bring water from the Gila River to the lands at Toltec. It was found, however, that the damsite on the Gila River had been filed upon by a millionaire furniture manufacturer from Grand Rapids, Michigan. Mr. Greene tried to get him to merge with the Santa Cruz Reservoir and Land Company, but he refused to do so. I was then instructed by Mr. Greene to shut

Oregon. However, I knew if I was to stay I would have to equip myself for some job different than cattle, so I took a course in salesmanship under a Mr. Prentis in Portland. After several weeks in this course, the Union Oil Company had asked the Prentis school to recommend a man to them who would develop into a salesman. Prentis recommended me and I went to work for the Union Oil Company. I worked for them about three years, had been promoted to Tank Truck Superintendent and salesman-at-large, that is, I was the only salesman not confined to a definite territory; I was free to cover the entire city.

As my heart was always in the cattle business, I was constantly looking for a good grass range where we could start a little spread and have room to expand. We found such a spot in what was known as the Little Cove on the east side of the Deschutes River in Wasco County, Oregon. This was open range country with plenty of grass and water, but very rough. We filed on three hundred and twenty acres of land, at the land office in The Dalles, then returned to Portland to work a few months more for the oil company before moving out to the homestead.

Just before leaving, I went out to see Dad Thornton who was running a garage at 13th and Hawthorne in Portland. He said he just naturally had to continue in the livery stable business no matter what it led to, and he could see very little difference between taking care of a horse or an automobile. Both demanded just so much attention and both, in equal degree, showed lack of attention to the gloss of their coats, whether the coat be hair or paint. As Dad always loved a well-groomed horse, his care of automobiles brought him many customers. As we were both oldtimers, Dad and I, and both old cowhands, we had much in common, but somehow I never could get him loosened up enough to speak of the past. I knew Dad had seen a lot of life and knew the West from Omaha to the Pacific. One day in our conversation I mentioned a saloon in Pearce, Arizona, way back in the ninety's, and Dad got started. It was then that Dad told me a very interesting story about Young Clark's emerald, as follows.

"That reminds me," says Dad, "that it's damn easy to get into the saloon business at times, even when you least expect it.

"In the early ninety's, I was working for the 4-Bar outfit in Montana. It was in the fall of the year and we had finished gathering a trainload of steers for the Omaha market. After several days of slow trailing from the range we arrived at the shipping point on the Great Northern.

"My bed pardner was a cowhand by the name of Jack Marshall. Jack was not only a top hand but he was one of the best singlehanded poker players in Montana and was happiest when seated with his feet under the round table with a stack of chips in front of him and his hat pulled down over his eyes. You've seen 'em, haven't you—keep their hats pulled down so you can't get a square look at 'em and tell when they're bluffing?

"We found the cars all ready with a train crew on the job, so it didn't take us long to get those critters aboard and on their way. After loading out we was to spend the night in town, load up with grub for the headquarters ranch and pull for home. The outfit left on time the following day, but Jack and I didn't go with it. We had to remain in town and take care of our business.

"You see it was this way. As soon as supper was over, Jack started looking for a poker game. There was only one saloon in the place and the proprietor was running his own game. When Jack and I sets in we buys a twenty dollar stack apiece and spreads about a hundred in bills in front of us. The rule was a man could play what was in front of him and no more. This was to keep a fellow from taking too much advantage of a good hand. The sky was the limit with what you had in front of you. You could buy in again after getting cleaned out, but you showed down for what you had on the table.

"Well, we plays until two o'clock in the morning, and the game ended with Jack having all the saloonkeeper's money and six hundred and fifty dollars of signed IOU's. The proprietor steps over to the cash register, takes out a twenty dollar bill, turns the keys over to Jack, puts on his coat and hat and walks out, and Jack and I found ourselves with a saloon on our hands, stocked with about six hundred dollars worth of liquor of different kinds. We locks up and goes out to the wagon and rolls in.

"The next morning we found a bunch of the boys with a hangover and dying for a drink. They had found the saloon locked, located the proprietor, who informed them that the saloon belonged to Jack and me, and it hadn't taken 'em long to get us out of bed to open up. We figured we would stay open long enough to sell out the supply of whiskey on hand and then pull for the ranch, but we found you can never figure for sure when in the saloon business. The following day the freight unloads five barrels of whiskey and two dozen cases from a wholesale house in Butte, same having been ordered some two weeks before by the old owner. We debates about taking this shipment but as business seemed to be good and we was cleaning up about twenty dollars each day, we stayed open. It looked pretty good to two forty-dollar-a-month cowhands.

"About every six months Jack used to take a trip into Butte to pay our bills and to try out his hand with the professional gamblers, and just as regular he would come back with from six hundred to fifteen hundred dollars of their money. One day he returns from one of his trips to Butte and has two beautiful stick pins, one a diamond, and the other an emerald, 'Thornton,' he says, 'I won both of these from young Clark and there's eight hundred dollars apiece due on each one. I am leaving the emerald with you and if young Clark ever redeems it, be sure and collect eight hundred bucks from him.'

"Well, we stays in that little town for about four-and-a-half years. Business prospered. We built a new saloon building, bought the hotel from old lady McLain, and finally sold out our holdings for seventeen thousand five hundred dollars. We divided that. Jack joined in the Alaska rush a few years after and died up in the north country somewhere. The emerald had never been redeemed by young Clark, and I kept it in remembrance of my old pardner, Jack Marshall.

"A few years later found me running a bunch of horses and one day in Butte, while passing a jewelry and secondhand store owned and operated by a Jew named Solomon, I saw in the window a veterinary surgeon's instrument kit, which I needed, so I steps into the store to find out the price of it. Old Solomon comes forward and I pointed to the case in the window and asked its price. I was wearing the emerald in my tie at the time. As soon as old Solomon saw it he became very excited. 'Where did you get that stone?' he asked. I told him it had been given to me by my old pardner, who had won it in a poker game from young Clark.

"May I see it?" he asked. "Sure," I told him, "if you stand right where you are you may look at it, but don't get funny.' "My dear man," says old Solomon, "everybody in Montana knows me. You need not hesitate to let me look at it. All I want to do is to determine if it is a genuine emerald."

I screwed the pin out of the tie—it was one of the old-fashioned screw kind—and handed it to him. Solomon adjusted a glass to one eye and examined the under side of the stone, found some marks and, after turning to a book he had, said the stone had been sold to young Clark by Tiffany of New York in April, 1892. He was satisfied it was genuine emerald.

"Now," says Solomon, "I want to know what you will take for the stone." "I do not want to sell it," I replied. "It's all I have to remember old Jack by. I never intend to part with it as long as I have a dollar to eat with." Solomon then said that he had an order for a brooch which called for a large emerald for the centerpiece, and he offered me eighteen hundred dollars for the stone. Well, eighteen hundred was a lot of money, but I thought too much of old Jack to part with it so I refused to sell.

"Here is the emerald—if you care to look at it," said Dad, and raising up a pocket lapel on his old army shirt, he showed me the largest emerald I have ever seen. "As long as I live," said Dad, unless it is a matter of life or death, I will never part with Jack's emerald." Should you ever run onto Dad Thornton in the Idaho country, you will find him still true to the memory of his old pardner, and under the lapel on his old shirt will be found the Clark emerald.

Life on the Homestead

When we finally arrived at our homestead in Wasco County, we set to work building our first cabin. It was necessary to pack in several rolls of heavy asphalt paper and by using alder for poles we were able to put up a frame, to which we tacked the paper and soon had a comfortable place in which to live. In addition to a No. 7 wood stove we had packed in a Singer sewing machine and an old time Victor phonograph. We also had brought with us from Portland a cage of four little canaries—a pair and their youngsters. The canary cage was suspended from the roof by a wire and was quite close to the outside wall, hanging just above the sewing machine, on top of which was the phonograph.

One day we had been out riding the range since early

morning and got to the cabin about four in the afternoon. The first thing we noticed when entering the cabin
was that the cage contained only one canary. We were at
a loss to understand what had happened—no sign of any
disturbance, no loose feathers, nothing. I immediately cut
sign around the cabin, thinking that somebody had taken
the birds; no tracks except our own were to be found. I
went out to the woodpile and was cutting up some wood
for the stove when I heard the Missus call. Dropping the
axe, I rushed back to the cabin. We had a long butcher
knife with a blade at least sixteen inches in length, a
regular machete. I found the Missus standing over the
phonograph which was on top of the sewing machine,
with the heavy knife in her hand. She pointed to the
phonograph and said, "There is a snake under it—you
raise the phonograph and I'll get the snake." Well I
grabbed the phonograph and raised it up, and the Missus
cut the darn sewing machine in two right down the
middle, but she got the snake. Here was the culprit—it
had managed in some way to get the canaries in the cage.

Our homestead was located in the middle of the holdings of Ewen MacLennan, an old country Scotchman,
who ran about 1000 head of mixed cattle and four bands
of sheep. I soon found in talking with neighboring homesteaders that they were all of them ordering MacLennan
to keep his sheep off their land. It was the first time for
most of them to have a place of their own and they were
too quick to assert their ownership. MacLennan came
riding by one day and I told him to cross my land whenever he found it necessary, for I had no intention of
bothering his rights as long as my land was unfenced. In a
few days one of his packers, in passing, left a hindquarter
of mutton as a gift from Mr. MacLennan.

One morning early we were awakened by a lot of

shouting as if someone was driving stock. I caught up my saddle horse and rode out to find out what was going on. I found MacLennan and his men, all Scotchmen, just driving a bunch of cows and calves into a large sheep corral intending to brand the calves. I rode up and watched them build a fire and lay on the branding irons. The irons were soon hot and they started to rope the calves. On account of the corral being so large, it was almost impossible for them to be able to reach the calves with their ropes and when they did they were unable to catch a calf. I took my rope and, entering the corral, asked if I could help them; they said I could if I wanted to. I then told them to run the stock by me and when they did I would rope a calf for them. In this way I roped all of the twenty-eight calves and the branding was soon over. MacLennan thanked me for my help, saying that I was a grand cowboy.

Several days later MacLennan came by leading a horse; said he had a carload of steers which he had bought down at the shipping corral at the railroad which was about one-and-a-half miles down the canyon, and asked me if Wylie, my son, and I would go down and brand them for him, stating that he had brought the extra horse for Wylie to ride. Also he said that a young man named Orville Higgins was already at the corral and had the branding irons for the job. We rode down and found twenty-six 2-year-old steers, and Higgins in the corral. It was hard work, as the horses were not trained to rope off so we had to handle them on foot. I would catch a steer by the head and immediately take a hitch around a corral post, then catch one hind leg and in this way get it down and tied so we could get it branded. It was a tough job and took us until dark to get all twenty-six steers branded.

In a few days MacLennan came by and asked me to work for him, to look after his cattle only, not to have anything to do with the sheep. So I went to work for MacLennan. My working for him meant that I would be away from the homestead during the week, returning home every Saturday night. The Missus' brother, Will Burruss had joined us, so she was not left alone on the homestead. In due time by using a four-horse team of MacLennan's we were able to haul in enough lumber to build a three-room cabin of our own. Unknown to me, the Missus and her brother had decided to build a fireplace; by working hard, with Bill hauling the rock on a sled from a ledge of flat rock down the canyon, and the Missus mixing the mud and laying the rock, they were able to finish the fireplace before Saturday and with a fire already laid were going to surprise me when I rode in Saturday evening. The great moment arrived—they could see me coming down the ridge when I was about a quarter of a mile away, so Bill rushed in and lit the fire. When I arrived, smoke was pouring out all the windows and doors and Bill and the Missus had been driven out of the house into the yard. This was a great disappointment to my wife; an examination of the chimney showed that she had not put the necessary gooseneck into the fireplace which is necessary before any fireplace chimney will draw properly.

I got to be quite a favorite of Mr. MacLennan and most every evening he asked me to join him in his library where we would discuss current events and things in general. On one of these evenings he told me about the Battle of the Basket. In the year 1895, in the southern part of Wasco County, a situation had developed which was causing considerable worry to the old Scotchman, a situation which was fast approaching a climax. Ewen

MacLennan was running three bands of sheep on a range covering several thousand acres of prime grazing lands, acreage controlled by small plots of patented lands located in such a position on scattered springs and watering places as to control these areas.

For years he had enjoyed the use of his range, but lately his neighbors to the north had started to encroach on his spread and MacLennan was worried. He knew he was going to have to put up a fight to protect his holdings, a fight which could develop into a serious range war in which a number of men might be killed.

The Connolly's who were old country Irish, joined MacLennan's range to the north; Hinton to the east, and Fisher to the south. A showing of weakness could easily develop into a loss of a large part of his holdings. Just how to protect his range without serious trouble was the problem to be solved.

It was the custom of sheepmen in the early days to trail their bands to summer ranges in the higher mountains where the sheep would spend the hot summer months. In order for the Connolly's to do this they were compelled to trail across MacLennan's range from north to south. It was also the custom rigidly adhered to by most sheepmen to keep the bands moving when crossing a neighbor's range and not allow the sheep to spread out and slow-graze his grass. The Connolly's always kept their bands moving when on their way to summer ranges, but on the return trip they had the habit of letting them spread out when approaching their home range and graze off the north end of MacLennan's holdings, usually dropping into and through "The Basket" camp, using Mac-Lennan's corrals and cabin for a night or two.

"The Basket" was so named on account of its topography being a series of ridges lying like the fingers of a hand, these ridges all converging into the main canyon near and around the small plot of level land where the cabin and corrals were placed. Encroaching on The Basket was getting to be a common practice, and Mac-Lennan's herders, after working slowly through the range, often upon arrival found The Basket well grazed off. Mac-Lennan had stood for this situation as long as he could and was determined to make a stand against the Connolly's, but was worried just how this could be done without a fight between his men and theirs.

The sheep were making their return from the summer range, MacLennan's bands had already arrived on the home range, and the Connolly's were on the return trail. The old man, all summer long, had been racking his brain trying to find some way to stop the Connolly's without bloodshed. At some time during the summer months he had worked out a plan. He visited his three herders, Morrison, MacGinnis, and MacIntosh, and outlined his plan. His packer, Malcolm MacDonald, was also instructed in the part he was going to play. He requested all to watch closely the Connolly sheep when passing through and report immediately to him should the Connolly's drop into The Basket. "Do not report any other violations—I am only interested should they attempt to graze The Basket." The old man had carefully gone over his entire holdings and picked The Basket on account of its many ridges as the place to make his stand, for behind these ridges he could hide his bands of sheep. Morrison's band was at the Moe Camp; MacGinnis' at Upper Two Springs, and MacIntosh's, when the call came, at Wells Pasture on the Deschutes River.

MacDonald, his packer, located the Connolly sheep in The Basket about two o'clock in the afternoon, noticed that the herder was using the cabin, which meant the

Connolly band intended to remain overnight. Under the plan which had been outlined, MacDonald rode down to the Moe Camp and started Morrison's band towards The Basket, then on to Upper Two Springs, and started Mac-Ginnis' to The Basket. All these drives were made at night. MacDonald then made a run for the home ranch to advise MacLennan. From the Moe Camp to The Basket is about a six or seven hour drive; figuring Morrison would get started about four in the afternoon, they estimated he would arrive near The Basket around midnight. Morrison was instructed to stop his band about a mile from The Basket and wait for further orders. MacGinnis, from Upper Two Springs, had the longer drive—it was estimated he should arrive about daylight. Each herder was instructed to carry lunch enough for two meals.

The moment MacDonald arrived with the news, the old man went into action—MacDonald was to change horses and return to help Morrison; Jesse Black, with a pack outfit and grub, was started immediately to move MacIntosh to Chicken Springs, which was northwest of The Basket, and between the latter and Connolly's range. It was figured that MacIntosh would not be in position until noon the next day; he was to establish camp at Chicken Springs, then swing his band east so as to place him just north of The Basket and between there and Connolly's range. With Morrison just below The Basket, MacGinnis just above, and MacIntosh to the north, Mac-Lennan would have Connolly surrounded.

MacLennan lined up another pack string with grub, blankets and other equipment, took Jim Baxter to do the cooking, and rode to overtake MacGinnis. He got off his horse, went in and asked the herder what he was doing with his sheep on his range, using his cabin, and the like. The herder could not answer, but advised that as soon as his packer arrived he would move out. MacLennan ordered him off, rode down the canyon, turned to his left, and located Morrison. As Morrison's band was in the best position for the attack, the band was moved into position about a half mile from The Basket canyon, just out of sight from the cabin.

Connolly's herder let his sheep out of the corral while he finished his breakfast, but before he could finish, Morrison attacked. MacLennan immediately mixed their bands with the Connolly sheep. Under the custom of the range it is necessary to move both bands to the nearest corral, there to be separated. This was done, and by this time Baxter had arrived, set up camp and got breakfast for the outfit. Considerable delay was arranged and it was rather late in the morning before the separating started.

The plan here called for the MacLennan sheep to be put on the outside in separating; in this way the Connolly sheep would be kept inside without feed and water. MacLennan's men immediately went to work and before the Connolly herder realized what was taking place, a bunch of MacLennan sheep were already on the outside. As sheep are marked with a large brand on their backs and also earmarked, it is fairly easy to tell ownership, but in the absence of a chute where the work must be done by hand, it is a long hard job. The bands were separated about four in the afternoon. In the meantime, the Connolly packer had arrived but turned around and left to notify the Connolly's what was taking place. After the separation, Morrison's band was moved out to graze, and MacGinnis' band was moved into position, Connolly's herder, as soon as possible, let his band out of the corral but before he could get away, MacGinnis moved in and mixed him again. He was immediately turned back into the corral. It was too late to separate that night so both bands remained in the corral over night. During the night the Connolly men rode in.

Next morning the separating commenced again; with extra help of the Connolly men the bands were separated by two o'clock. This meant that the Connolly band had been in the corral two nights, one full day, and three-quarters of another day without feed and water. By this time the Connolly sheep were commencing to look rather gaunt.

Morrison's band was moved into position again when it was seen that the separating was about finished; Mac-Intosh was in sight to the north, ready to move in if commanded. When they turned out the Connolly sheep and Tom Connolly looked up and saw Morrison's fresh band moving in for the mix, he threw up his hands, ran up to MacLennan and promised he would never again bother MacLennan's range if they would let him out. Tom Connolly kept his promise. MacLennan waved Morrison's sheep away, and the setting sun that evening found Connolly's sheep high up on the hills to the north, making a night retreat from the "Battle of the Basket," and MacLennan had won his battle with no one injured.

I do not know whether Ewen MacLennan is still alive, but if he is you will find him surrounded with a library of the world's great battles, and he will tell you, as he often told me, that he 'has been in the wrong vocation all his life; that he should have been a military man." And true enough, here was a man who manipulated bands of sheep like generals handle armies of soldiers, and thereby solved his problem.

Range War

When the Blakely Clough Company bought the Ewen MacLennan holdings west of Shaniko, Blakely brought in his own men to head the two departments, sheep and cattle. A long, lanky six-footer named Art Summers took over the cattle work and I returned to my homestead in what was known as the Little Cove. The Little Cove had been used as a summer range for cattle by John and Eddie Bolter and the Veazie ranch on Hay Creek for over thirty years.

Willis Brown was the V Z ranch manager and meeting him one day in Madras, he asked me if I would go to work for him, stating that he was on a deal to lease part of the Warm Springs Indian Reservation and if the deal went through he wanted me to look after the Warm

Springs end of the ranch. I agreed to work for Brown and was immediately placed on the payroll. At the time Brown said he was getting ready to turn his cattle out on the lower river range and I could help with that work. Since I was homesteading in the Little Cove he said I could remain on the homestead until such time as he needed me on the Reservation. I told Brown that it would be necessary for me to return home in order to advise the Missus so she would not be worried and that I would be back on Hay Creek the following day. I explained the situation to her and the next morning caught up a fresh horse and reported to Brown that evening.

Bolters had already turned out their cattle on the Little Cove summer range. We started for the summer range with three hundred and fifty head of mixed V Z cattle, we stopped over night at Brown's Kaskella Ranch on the lower Deschutes River and headed for the Cove early the next morning. When we reached the other side of what we called The Pot, we picked up about a hundred head of Bolter's cattle and carrying them with us entered the Little Cove with about four hundred and fifty head in all. Evidently Blakely's man Summers saw us as we came over the hill and dropped into the Cove. As four hundred and fifty head cattle, if looked at well-strung out, would be guessed as twice the number, I was told later that Summers reported to the Blakely Company that I had brought in over a thousand head of cattle. As Blakely had been in possession of his new ranch for only a couple of weeks he was ignorant of range conditions and had no knowledge of actual range uses. However, I understand that Blakely was not at the ranch at the time and Summers was sure that I was trying to steal the range.

In proving up on a homestead it is compulsory for the homesteader to plough up and put to crop a certain percentage of his land. I had about thirty-five acres ploughed up and planted to rye, but had not been able to find time to fence it, so it was wide open. Whenever I was away riding the different parts of the range it was necessary for the Missus to keep a horse saddled and line ride this rye field to keep the cattle from grazing it down.

When I left Brown the day we put the cattle in the Cove he said I would need another horse. He instructed me to come up to Hay Creek in a day or so and he would have the boys put shoes on a bay horse he had and I could use him; told me I would find him a very good rope horse. A couple of days later I rode up to get this horse. The Missus stayed on the homestead, line-riding the cattle to keep them off the rye. It was a day's ride to Hay Creek—I had to stay overnight and did not get back into the Little Cove until late in the evening of the next day. When I started down the hill towards our cabin I heard someone calling and looking up the hill I saw one of Blakely's sheepherders whom I knew waving his hat for me to ride up to where he was. As it is a range custom never to turn down a call of this kind, I turned up the mountain and joined Lockey Morrison, the herder, and asked him if he was in trouble. He said not but told me that I was; that Summers had run a bunch of cattle over the Missus, said he had never seen such riding by any woman, fighting Summers to the finish and that if Summers had not had the additional help of his dog she would have won the battle. I thanked Lockey and asked him where Summers was camped. He told me he thought he was with the boys at the sheep camp. Blakely had a tent camp at what was called the Sheep Camp and had several of his men getting the corrals in shape, as lambing would start in a few days.

I rode down to the homestead and the Missus filled me in on the battle. She said what made her the maddest was that after fighting Summers back and forth until her horse played out, he stopped just as he left, raised up in his saddle and cheered over his victory. She hollered at him just as he left and told him the boss would look him up as soon as he returned. I handed the Missus the horse I was leading, never getting off my horse while talking to her, and started for the Sheep Camp. By this time it was dark and as I approached the tent I could see the shadows of several men flitting across the canvas walls of the tent. I dismounted a few yards away, tied my horse to a juniper tree and, jerking open the flap of the tent, jumped inside and asked which one of them was Summers, as I had never met him. Donald Morrison, whom I knew, said Summers had gone to the main ranch. "You mean to tell me after what he had done today he is not here?" I asked. "No," Donald said, "he has gone." I asked if anyone was going to the ranch that night and they told me one of the boys was going up after a supply of nails in order to finish the work on the lambing pens. I told this man to tell Summers to stay out of the Little Cove, that if I ever caught him there again I would settle with him. "Tell him he whipped a woman today, but he's up against a man now—and to stay out."

I realized that I was up against a range war, so after riding the Cove for a couple of days looking for Summers, I felt that in order to protect the V Z interests it might be necessary to lease land from some of the homesteaders who had taken up land in the Cove. So I rode to Hay Creek and laid the situation before Brown. He agreed that it would be advisable to lease some of the homesteads, supplied me with three blank checks signed by him and said he would back me to the limit. He remarked that they had used the Little Cove as a summer range for years and could well afford some extra expense to hold it.

I leased Sam Lease's homestead just north of and adjoining Boiling Springs in the Upper Cove, paying him the price he asked—fifty dollars for a year's lease. Before I got around to leasing more ground, I found Lockey Morrison grazing his sheep on Lease's homestead. I rode over and told Lockey that I had leased the place but for him to go on using it as I had no intention of keeping Blakely's stock off. While I was talking to Lockey, Blakely rode up; we sat down on the ground and had a long talk—I explained to him how the Bolter and Veazie cattle had been using the Little Cove for years for a summer range. Blakely thanked me for setting him right, said he would see that Summers left the cattle alone. "Well, Mart, I was sure things would be different if it was explained to you so I will call off the orders I have given Summers to stay out of The Cove—you can tell him he is free to ride in any time he finds it necessary; I will never bother him. He probably got excited when he saw the cattle being driven in and thought he was doing the right thing. His only mistake was when he found a woman riding to protect the rye field, he should have been gentleman enough to have immediately stopped." It seems Mart Blakely forgot to tell Summers that I had called off my part of the battle.

Another month had passed, lambing was over and cars had been set in at Cove Creek to haul the bands of sheep to Terrebonne; from there they would be trailed to their summer range. Blakely stopped to chat with us when passing the homestead, said they were loading out the first band for the mountains that day and he was on his way to join them. He said he would have to make the trip up with the sheep, to be gone for several days and that he should be there to get things started at cutting hay on the Two Springs ranch and he was short of men to do the work and a little worried. I volunteered to help out with the Two Springs haying—the war was on and men were hard to find—it was our duty to help. Our son was with us, so telling Blakely to go on with the sheep and forget it, the Missus, Wylie and I left immediately for Two Springs, the Missus to do the cooking for the haying crew. We loaded our bedding on the buckboard, started the Missus on her way with the outfit, Wylie and I going on horseback, which would bring us to Two Springs about a half hour ahead of the buckboard. When Wylie and I came in sight of the ranch, we saw a man in the stack yard who, upon looking up and seeing us, went in to the house. We saw him pick up something which he covered with his shirt as he started towards the house. What we did not know was that this man was Summers and that he had picked up a heavy bridge bolt. We opened the gate and rode in; the Missus was still behind us coming with the bedding. Stopping at the little horse shed, I told Wylie I would go in and let them know that we had come to help with the haying.

The Two Springs house had a screen door at the kitchen entrance. I stopped at the door and called helloo. I could see someone inside bending over the stove. Receiving no answer I opened the screen door and stepped inside. A man raised up from the stove—it was Summers —and with a long seven-eighths inch bridge bolt in his hands made a run for me. I ran in under the blow, taking it over my right shoulder; I immediately grabbed the bolt with one hand, raining blows on his head with my right hand—I had to hang on to the bolt. In our struggle we tipped over the table and a couple of chairs and realizing from the racket that I was in some kind of a fight, Wylie came rushing in. I yelled at him to grab up a stick of wood from the wood box and see if he could knock the fellow loose from the bolt. Wylie rapped Summers over the head; Summers with his back against the screen door immediately gave me a shove with the bolt, turned loose and fled out the door. As he rounded the corner of the house I threw the bolt and hit him in the back. Rounding the corner of the house, Wylie threw his stick of wood at Summers hitting him in the back of the head, but as the stick was cottonwood no harm was done. The Missus had not yet arrived. Summers kept running to where Carlin and Thompson were working in the hay field. Wylie and I walked over to the horse shed; just as we reached it, Wylie called my attention to two men running towards us from the field carrying pitchforks. I had picked up the bolt and stepped into the shed and found a pitchfork there. I brought it out and standing the bolt and pitchfork up against the shed, I told Wylie that I would walk out to meet the two men and try to talk to them; if I failed to reason with them I would call to him and he was to grab whichever weapon he preferred and I would take what he left. I told him we were not going to be run off and for him not to hesitate to hurt these fellows if we had to fight them. When the men got close enough to see them well, I could see that both were badly out of wind on account of the long run; so turning to Wylie I called attention to this and said we would not have much trouble handling the pair.

Carlin and Thompson, the two men, came up all out of breath and asked what was going on. I told them that Blakely had asked us to come down to help with the haying and the Missus would do the cooking. At this moment Summers came driving up with the hayrack, so nodding at him, I stated that the man had tried to kill me with a bridge bolt and we had to work him over a little. Summers had tied the team and came rushing out to join Carlin and Thompson. He asked Carlin, who seemed to be the boss, if he wasn't going to do something. Carlin's reply took all the wind out of Summers' sails, "Hell, no! I'm not going to lose two good men and a cook in order to keep one poor worker."

The Missus arrived at that time so we busied ourselves in getting the buckboard unloaded. Summers immediately went to saddle up his horse, getting ready to leave. I went into the shed and tried to talk with him, but he was too badly worked up to talk. He left as soon as his horse was saddled and I am sure that the poor devil firmly believed that I was after him on account of the way he had treated the Missus, and I am also sure that Mart Blakely never told Summers that the battle had been called off. One can sometimes get into serious trouble when he does not expect it.

Summers never stopped until he reached Condon and after he learned the truth about things was always bitter toward Blakely for not telling him that I had called off the battle. Western men have always had great respect for their women—I think Blakely was disgusted with Summers for staging the fight with the Missus and purposely forgot to tell him the whole story. Anyway when Blakely returned from the trip up to the summer range with the sheep, he found the Two Springs hay put up and we were back on the homestead.

Time marched on and I often met Blakely; during one of these meetings he told me of his trouble with the Shaniko Ranch employees. It seems that his foreman by the name of Damms was very much disliked and the men in talking with Blakely had advised him of this fact and some were threatening to leave. As men were scarce he was of course worried and told me he guessed he would have to let Damms go as soon as he could find a man to replace him. During this talk I advised him if he did put in another foreman, to discharge the entire crew and let the new man rehire them, then stay away from the men, and hold the new foreman responsible, for when the owner is too friendly with the crew, one usually has labor trouble. I had talked with some of his crew and found out that Blakely's friendliness was the cause of most of the trouble. He had also developed a situation that would cause trouble for any new foreman. When the men had complained to Blakely about Damms he usually responded with the remark, "I guess I will have to replace Damms, but can not find a suitable man at the moment."

There were three different departments on the ranch; the farm which was responsible for the hay crop, the cattle which called for someone familiar with the cattle, and the sheep which required an understanding of the sheep business. Three different employees had approached Blakely, brought up the subject of Damms and told him that he did not need a general foreman, that they were well qualified to handle it; Roy Reynolds for the farm, Bob Thompson for the cattle and Bob Carlin for the sheep. Blakely agreed immediately that each one was qualified for his particular position and while he did not say the jobs would be theirs he did leave them with the thought that he was agreeable.

My son Wylie was working on the ranch with the hay crew which was busily haying at the time. Wylie showed up at the homestead about dark one evening and said Blakely wanted me to come to the ranch at once and take charge. I remembered the talk I had with him about someone replacing Damms, but I did not have any idea from this talk that he had me under consideration. I asked Wylie if Blakely was at the ranch and he replied that he was not, but had gone to The Dalles and would be back some time the next day; also that he had instructed Damms to turn the outfit over to me.

I saddled up, left the Missus on the homestead and left for the ranch arriving about ten in the evening. I located Damms who verified that I was to take charge and that under instructions from Blakely he had paid off the entire crew and that most of them expected to pull out early the next morning. By this time it was eleven o'clock and meant that I would have to move fast or the ranch would be without a crew in the morning. I asked Damms for a list of the employees and scanning over the names I noted that a man I knew named George Stage was included. I asked Damms where Stage was sleeping, woke him up, explained the situation and asked him just what position he was holding on the crew. Stage said he was stacking, which is a rather important position on a hay crew, for a good stacker can put up a stack of hay that will stand the weather and save you money by doing so. I asked George what he was being paid and he told me two-fifty per day. I told him to get up and help me hire back the crew, that from now he was in charge of the hay crew and his wages would be raised to three dollars. Stage and I woke the crew and all agreed to continue on. Roy Reynolds was in the hay crew and agreed to stay on. The two Bobs, Thompson and Carlin, were down at the Two Springs on the river and were in a way not directly under Damms at the time.

Blakely did not get back to the ranch until late afternoon; by that time everything was progressing nicely and

I was busy taking an inventory of kitchen supplies to know just what was on hand and what was needed to keep a crew of men happy.

The next day a fellow by the name of Art Henderson showed up at the ranch and asked if he could ride the range looking for some of Fargeth's cattle, stating he was riding for Fargeth who owned a ranch north of the Mac-Lennan Ranch in the Bake Oven Country. I designated a pasture for Henderson to use, should he find any Fargeth cattle and explained that I could not help him ride, but that I would help him with the cattle when he started back. Henderson fooled around for about a week during which he had ridden down to the Two Springs Ranch and stayed one night with the two Bobs. One morning he told me he had three head of Fargeth cattle and would like to start back with them and asked me to help him. We went out into the pasture, rounded up the three head and started down Deep Creek which runs into the Bake Oven just below the Fargeth ranch. This was rough country where the cattle did not cause any trouble, but it was necessary for me to stay with Henderson until he was clear of our cattle range and on the Connolly sheep range. While riding alongside him, he several times made the remark that he wished he could be at the Blakely Ranch on Sunday. As this was Saturday, I asked him why he would not stay over Sunday. He stated he had been in-structed to return that day and they would be looking for him. He however kept mentioning the fact that he wished he could stay over until out of curiosity I insisted on knowing what was going to happen on Sunday. He then told me that the two Bobs were coming up, were going to join up with Reynolds and would run me off the ranch. He also told me that Blakely in a way had promised them the outfit, Reynolds the farm, Thompson the cattle, and

Carlin the sheep, and that they were plenty mad when Blakely brought me in to run the outfit.

I thanked Henderson for the information, turned back when we reached the sheep range and rode back to the Ranch. I had of course brought the Missus up from the homestead and she was in charge of the headquarters residence; we had a cook for the haying crew but the Missus was helping a Mrs. Favor with the cooking. When I got in, I told my wife what Henderson had said and asked her to get the information to me, should the two Bobs show up. I had made arrangements to meet a rancher named Newcombe whose ranch joined us on the east. Blakely found that an eighty we owned jogged into Newcombe and that he had an eighty which jogged into us. An agreement had been made to trade eighties and Newcombe and I were to flag out the fence lines.

When I rode by the hay crew, the boys were putting up the gin pole for a new stack, having moved over that morning to another hay ground. The cook cabin for the hay crew was mounted on a wagon and usually followed the crew from pasture to pasture, as this was wild hay which we were cutting. Newcombe and I were busy flagging out the fence line when I observed my son riding toward us and riding as if in a hurry. My first thought was that the gin pole had fallen and someone was hurt. I walked out to meet Wylie whose first words were, "Dad, they're here."

"What are you talking about?" I asked.

"The two Bobs." Then I understood.

"How did you get word?"

"Mother rode out."

"Where is Mother?"

"She is at the stack yard. I have her horse."

I told Newcombe that something had happened which

was calling me away, for him to go on with the flagging and I left with Wylie for the stack yard. I asked where the two Bobs were—Mother passed them at the cook wagon. I had noticed that Reynolds had his horse saddled when I passed the hay crew. I told Wylie to come with me and that Mother would need the horse he was riding. So I planned to ask Reynolds to loan me his horse and if he refused we would take it anyway and ride to meet the two Bobs. When I asked Reynolds for his horse, he readily agreed to my taking him. This eliminated Reynolds, leaving the two Bobs still to be met.

The cook wagon had not been moved but was still set up on the road to Shaniko; as we rode over the hill and came in sight of the wagon the two Bobs were just leaving to join Reynolds at the stack. They looked up and saw the Missus, Wylie and me approaching and instead of turning to their left to go around the fence corner, they continued up the Shaniko Road which put the fence line between them and us. We got off our horses and crawled through the fence. I told Wylie I would walk out into the road to stop them; for him to stay out of it unless he saw I was getting the worst of it, then stack in with everything he had, cautioning him not to hesitate to hurt one of them if he had to, as no one was going to run us off the ranch.

I reached the road when the boys were about seventy-five yards away, still coming on horseback. One of my spurs rattled and on account of the ground being covered with sagebrush which would catch the spurs and possibly trip me, I realized it would be better not to have them on, so knelt down in the road to take them off. As the Bobs came closer, I walked to meet them; my wife and son were seated on a little knoll waiting to see what would happen. As I met the men I started talking, told them I understood they had ridden up with the intention of running me off the ranch and if they would get down one at a time I would find out just how good they were. Both denied that the visit was anything but friendly, that they had no notion of making trouble. I was just congratulating myself on the easy victory when my wife joined in. Walking up alongside me she said, "Do you boys mean to say that I have ridden all the way out here and I'm not going to see a fight?" I tried to stop her— here I had the situation in hand but after having her say, she gave a shrug of her shoulders as if to say, "What kind of men are these" and turned her back towards the horses. I was thankful that the two Bobs did not accept her challenge. My advice is never marry a Texan woman—she has peculiar ideas about a man's courage and loves a good honest fight.

Blakely discharged the two Bobs; they had never been turned over to me, and afterwards in Maupin some of the natives were kidding Bob Carlin about letting Axford bluff him out. Bob's answer was, "We might have licked Axford, but that damn woman of his would have killed both of us if we had."

Some Early-Day Characters

While working for the Blakely Clough Company I often met Billy Hunt who ran a couple of bands of sheep in the brakes of the Deschutes River. Hunt was quite a man, and for years had owned and operated Hunt's ferry across the Deschutes River at Maupin, Oregon, a little settlement on the west bank of the river. This ferry was for years the only means for the ranchers to cross the river with wagons and stock; wagons on their way to The Dalles for supplies and bands of sheep, cattle and horses on their way to summer pasture or to market. When the railroad came and a bridge was built across the river, Hunt located a homestead and went into the sheepraising business, running one or two bands of sheep on the open range southeast of Maupin, and in a few years was one of Wasco County's well-known sheepmen.

Hunt was a staunch Republican, strong in his opinions and always ready to back them up with a bet. The political year arrived in which feeling ran strong between the two political parties; Hughes had been nominated by the Republican Party to oppose the College Professor, Woodrow Wilson. The month of November had arrived and the day of the election was approaching. For several days Hunt had been badgering the Wilson supporters to place a bet on their man. A few bets had been made, but most of the citizens had doubts about the unknown teacher beating Hughes who had been in political life for several years and of course was well known.

Election day arrived and Hunt, provoked by the refusal of the Democrats to bet on Wilson, filled a bucket with cash and sitting on a chair in the middle of the street, batered everyone who passed, for a wager, the bucket filled with money at his side. The following day the returns showed that Hughes had been elected and the few who had bet on Wilson paid up. That evening a report came in that it was possible that Wilson had won but it would take the count of California's vote to settle the question. A number of those who had already settled their bets with Hunt asked for their money back until the election was decided for sure. This aroused Hunt who could not believe that Hughes had been defeated, that the rumors going around were not supported by facts. So, taking his chair and his bucket of money he again placed himself in the middle of the street and offered odds on Hughes to win. Hunt stood ready to mortgage his holdings and bet the pile on his judgment.

Fortunately for Billy Hunt, no one had the nerve to call him for when the votes of California were counted it showed that Wilson was the winner. I'll wager that Billy Hunt shuddered for years every time he thought about his narrow escape and many a resident of Maupin blamed himself for not having nerve enough to bet against him.

Today the Hunt Livestock Company is under the able management of Clarence Hunt, a son of Billy's, who is proving himself to be a chip off the old block, with this difference—Clarence is placing his bets on new improvements, new blood for his cattle, and the like, and is winning every bet.

It was at this time also that I was told about one of Wasco County's great mysteries—what happened to Veazie. This is how the story went. It was somewhere in the 1880's—the place, a road on the way to The Dalles, a town located in Wasco County, Oregon. In the early days ranchers owning holdings in Central Oregon usually made about two trips a year into The Dalles for supplies for this was before the coming of the railroad into Central Oregon and all transportation was by means of horse and wagon. It was customary when a rancher was going to make a trip for supplies to notify his neighbors and also bring out for them anything needed. The trips were usually made in a four-horse outfit with a good three-and-a-half inch wagon, as supplies of staples necessary to last six months or better were always bulky and heavy.

Old man Veazie who had large holdings on a small stream known as Hay Creek just above where this creek runs into Trout Creek, was getting ready to make a trip into The Dalles and had notified his neighbors of the proposed trip. Veazie had been a rancher on Hay Creek for several years and branded his cattle with one of the most suitable brands I have ever encountered in my many years of range work. The brand spelled out the name of the owner, Veazie, with two letters, V Z. I was told that two or three adjoining neighbors (and understand that what was called a neighbor in those days might live twenty or twenty-five miles away) had ridden over with a list of a few things they needed and had given Veazie money to pay for the supplies needed. The Veazie family consisted of his wife and two young sons. I do not know if there were other children or not, as the story as told to me mentioned only two sons.

Veazie pulled out early one morning driving a four-horse outfit, the family watched until the wagon was out of sight, then turned back to the house, not realizing that they would never see him again. Veazie had often made the trip into The Dalles and had always returned. But this time he did not come back and about a week later his wagon was found on the road at a point about where the old Maxwell ranch is now located on the old road to The Dalles. The wagon was on the return trip loaded with supplies, three of the team were tied to the wagon, one horse was missing. On the seat of the wagon was found the purchase list of the neighbors with the exact change with each list.

To this day it is not known what happened to Veazie. Here was a man fairly well to do with a happy family and a bright future who had ridden out of the town into the unknown. This man was respected by all, a good neighbor, and today it is still one of the mysteries of Central Oregon—what happened to Veazie. It is said that two exceptionally well dressed strangers were seen earnestly talking with Mr. Veazie in The Dalles. Was Veazie a member of some noble family and being called back? It was evident that he was above the average in breeding and education. Well, you take it from here. Nobody knows.

One of the men working under me at the Blakely Clough ranch was Blakely's brother-in-law, Lloyd Cauhorn. Lloyd was a big six-foot rawboned sort of a man weighing in the neighborhood of two hundred pounds—almost too big to be riding the range as a cowhand. My height was five feet nine and it crowded me to lower the beam to one hundred and fifty-eight pounds with all my clothes on. Cauhorn and I were riding the lower range just above Maupin on the Deschutes River where we were wintering a bunch of cows, checking things to find out how the cattle were doing. When we approached Chicken Springs where a man of ours had his camp, we were surprised to find on the low hills to the north a bunch of Connolly's sheep. This was an infringement of our rights, for the watering places and the range belonged to our company. Riding up to the herder, I asked him what he was doing with the sheep on our range and ordered him to get off the land. He called attention to a man approaching, leading a pack horse and said he was the packer and to talk to him. We turned and rode to meet the packer.

A packer for a band of sheep keeps the herder supplied with grub, helps to move the herder to another camping place and stays in readiness to relieve the sheepherder if he becomes sick or disabled. Because the sharp hoofs of the sheep, and as they usually keep close together when driven in and out of the camp ground, would soon destroy the grass, so bands of sheep are kept constantly on the move from one camp to another. About five or six days is as long as a good sheepman will leave a band in a camp.

We rode up to the packer and found him to be a big burly old country Irishman, weighing easily two hundred pounds or better, from the looks of his shoulders. I talked very plainly to the packer—in fact a little rough, and ordered him to move the sheep off immediately. This he promised to do. As we were riding along after leaving the packer, Cauhorn turned to me and asked, "What would you have done, Joe, if he had got down and pawed a hole in the ground?" "Why, Lloyd," I replied, "you didn't think I was going to fight him, did you? I was only trying to get him on the ground for you—he was just your size."

One day when down on the river, I dropped in to say hello to old Charlie U'Ren. Charlie and his Missus had an alfalfa field on the river and were milking a few cows. We were sitting alongside the house in the shade discussing things in general when the subject suddenly changed to physical ailments. Charlie had evidently been having trouble with his health for he started telling me about his afflictions. "Joe," he said, "I have considerable stomach trouble, some sinus trouble and a touch of bursitis in one shoulder." After going into considerable detail about his different ailments he suddenly turned to me saying, "You seem to be very healthy, Joe, don't seem to have any kind of sickness." I told him that my only trouble was low blood pressure. "What does that do to you?" asked Charlie. "The only difference I can see," I answered, "is that I seem to give out about three in the afternoon." "My God!" Charlie replied, "my blood pressure must be terribly low, as I give out about nine in the morning."

We Sell the Homestead

After selling our homestead to the Blakely Clough Company, I left Blakely and returned to Portland, went up one day to say hello to my friends in the Union Oil Office and was immediately put to work by Cecil Ireland, the assistant sales manager. I explained that it would be a week or ten days before I could report for work as I had promised Blakely to help with his income tax report. Ireland said, "I am putting you on the payroll today—you report to me as soon as you can, the sooner the better." When I reported for work about ten days later, I was sent to Vancouver, Washington, as relief man for the Agent there who was going on a two weeks vacation. When Lindsay, the agent, returned Ireland sent me to Astoria, as agent there; Kinzel the previous agent was put on sales.

When taking the monthly inventory, I found thirteen large 110-gallon drums of distillate in the plant, which should have been in the inventory. I asked Kinzel about this and he said the thirteen drums belonged to The Columbia River Packers Association, a large fish packing company operating on the Columbia and Alaskan rivers. I called them on the phone and told them I wanted them to take delivery of the thirteen drums as I needed the space. They called me back in a few minutes saying they had no record of the distillate belonging to them and that there must be some mistake. All refined oils for Oregon were brought in by company tankers from California. I had received notice from the Portland office that the tanker The Oleum would make a stop at Astoria and fill my tanks with refined oil. This was to be a night delivery, the neighborhood of course knew at once that we were going to take a night delivery, a couple of them complained about the night activities saying that while the ship was pumping, the night employees were busily rolling barrels around the plant and filling them, also sometimes filled the tank trucks. I felt sure that I now understood how the thirteen drums of distillate would be accounted for, but I waited to go through the routine of receiving the oil from the tanker before making my report to Portland.

Well, the boat arrived, the mate came up and took the gauges of the tanks, then returned to the ship and did not return until all ground tanks had been filled. I quickly saw that by filling barrels, trucks, etc. between gauging, cargo could be stolen from the ship without detection. I made my report to the Portland office, Mr. Victor Kelly, the Sales Manager, came down and I explained in detail how it was done, and showed him the thirteen drums of distillate which did not show in our inventories. Kelly instructed me to take in the distillate and stated this explains why tankers which had made the Astoria stop before continuing on to Portland always were short from 3000 to 5000 gallons after total delivery had been made at Portland. I put on a system of locks which completely stopped the thievery.

I remained in Astoria as Agent for two years, doubled the quantity of refined oils and increased the sale of lubricating oils and greases.

The Union Oil Company had built new plants at Ontario and Baker, Oregon, and it was in 1922 that I was sent to Baker to open up the territory for the company as Company Agent. Now, Baker County is a mineral country, then having several producing mines. In one of the Baker bank windows was a large display of ores from the different mines and, as many of Baker's early day mines were placer mines, a large part of the display was gold nuggets. In one small gold pan were several gold nuggets which were shaped like pumpkin seeds, worn smooth around the edges. A man had stopped alongside me and was also looking at the mineral display. "Look at those pumpkin seed nuggets; you can tell they have come a long way from where they originated; grinding on the bedrock has worn them smooth."

Immediately it flashed into my mind about the filigree nuggets which Gonzales had showed me; they must have originated right there in the lemon yellow dirt. The Mexican had probably not salted me. This bothered me for several days; finally I made an appointment to meet a Mr. W. C. Fellows who was a mining engineer in charge of a mine in the Granite Mining District. I told Fellows I was going to tell him about a prospect which a Mexican took me to once, and wanted him to give me his opinion. I explained that the deposit was lemon yellow, that the nuggets were of the filigree type and looked as clean and bright as if just made. He told me that the yellow deposit was tellurium oxidization; said this form of deposit was common in the Colorado mines. I called his attention again to the bright clean look of the nuggets. "Yes," Fellows said; "this proves it's a tellurium deposit; the elements, air and water together with acid which is in the rock, decompose the quartz; you dig down a few feet and you will come into your quartz vein." "Do you think I should look this over again?" I asked. "Well, there is usually only one chance in ten thousand for any showing to make a mine; I think you have a better than fifty-fifty chance."

Well, I made a trip down alone to Mexico in August 1924; found the San Tismo River high with flood water and raining every day. I had to turn back. I had a thirty-day furlough from the Oil Company; made the trip again in June 1947 with a neighbor, Bill Fehrenbacher, got as far as Batapelas when Bill took sick and I had to turn back with him. This lemon yellow deposit of dirt which Fellows said is tellurium oxidization is still there. Another lost gold mine. I found out just before I turned back with Fehrenbacher that no new gold discoveries had been made in the San Francisco Mountains for years.

In 1924 I was elected President of the Baker Kiwanis Club and became active in civic affairs and that year was also elected Vice-President of the Baker Chamber of Commerce. I got well acquainted with Walter Meacham who was the Secretary, and also President of The Old Oregon Trail Association. Learning that President Harding intended to make a trip through the Northwest, Meacham immediately saw an opportunity to advertise Oregon. After a meeting with the La Grande Chamber, they wired the President and his party, inviting the President to be their guest at Meacham on top of the Blue Mountains at the dedication of a monument to the memory of the early Oregon Trail pioneers, the monument to be placed at Emigrant Springs, a favorite camping place on the old trail.

President Harding accepted the invitation; Pendleton also joined in and arrangements were made to have a large number of Indians with their tepees set up when the President arrived. This was Pendleton's contribution. It was voted to have a pageant, a wagon trail to be got together, to have an Indian attack on the wagon train and a colorful parade, all for the entertainment of President Harding and his party. An old-time mining camp was to be built, with old time gambling, using imitation money. As they wanted to put on a show worth while for the President, it was soon found that the expense was going to run into several thousand dollars. It was agreed that a toll gate be built at both ends of the pageant grounds and one dollar per person admission charge made to help take care of the expense.

Will Calder and I were appointed to arrange for horses, wagons, stage coaches, etc. for the wagon train. We made arrangements with an old jerk-line teamster named Lentz to get a team together. The Baker fair grounds had several old time rigs and horses and drivers were found for them. With Ontario, Baker, Haines, North Powder, Union and La Grande all agreeing to have a wagon or two, it was soon seen that we were going to have a fairly large wagon train. At a joint meeting of the Kiwanis Club and the Chamber of Commerce, Will Calder got up and told of the progress of his committee and said it would be necessary to have a wagon Master to boss the train, as it would be traveling on the highway; with hundreds of automobiles passing someone who had an understanding of the handling of teams and men should be in charge. He remarked, "In working with Joe Axford on this committee, I have found that handling men and horses is an old story to Joe and I hereby make a motion that he be appointed the Wagon Boss." This was passed and I immediately took charge.

In order to control traffic on the highway it was necessary to have mounted men at both ends of the wagon train. As I intended to handle the front end of the train, it was necessary for me to have a horse that was not afraid of automobiles. Bill Polman had a pure white well-trained cow horse which he agreed I could use. I tried the horse out, found he was a well-reined horse and easily controlled. When Dollar Bill Ellis, who was to be Grand Marshall of the Pageant, saw me on the pure white horse he begged me to let him have the Polman horse and for me to find another one. I talked with Harry Lentz, a son of the jerk-line teamster who I had asked to handle the back end of the wagon train, and asked him to find another horse for me. Harry had a brown mare which I tried out and found I liked her better than the Polman horse for she had a much easier gait, so I turned the white horse over to Dollar Bill.

We started out from the Baker Fair Grounds and were to make our first night stop at Haines. I had driven over the entire route to be traveled by auto and had figured out where to stop each night and also where it was necessary to rest the teams before tackling a long hill ahead. Entering Haines I swung our seven or eight pieces of equipment, parking them in a small circle; here we were joined by another wagon. Immediately upon camping each driver was first to water and take care of the feeding of his stock. I also designated certain ones to rustle wood for the evening camp fires; the cooking had already been arranged for. The first evening we were joined around the campfire by a number of old timers living over again their earlier days.

At daybreak the next morning the stock was fed and watered and immediately after breakfast we were ready to roll. As most of the horses were not only soft but borrowed for the trip, it was necessary to take advantage of the cool morning hours for traveling. At North Powder were added a couple more covered wagons. At the foot of a long hill just before entering Union, I stopped the wagons to rest the teams for a couple of hours and for lunch. It was the 2nd of July and the days were a little warm for stock that had not been hardened. Old man Lentz and his boy Harry came up and joined me at lunch. Old Lentz was an old freighter and it was here at the foot of the hill that he paid me this compliment. "Axford," he said, "I have seen you often around Baker, always with a white collar on and I wondered why a white-collared man had been chosen as Wagon Boss, but I want to tell you that I have changed my first opinion. You sure know your business."

We rolled through Union and made another stop in LaGrande where we were again joined by a number of old timers. It was necessary to move on to the foot of a hill several miles long on the Grand Ronde which I had picked for the night stop. Here I was joined for a moment by Walter Meacham. Walter stated that someone, no doubt jealous of our entertaining the President, had wired the President that it was the intention to commercialize the President's visit by charging admission to the grounds, and they had wired that if this was done to cancel the President's visit; it was therefore necessary to do away with the toll gate and admit everyone without charge.

"Joe," he said, "we will be several months, if not a year or two paying for this."

About dusk a photographer by the name of Sills came by, asked who was in charge and, addressing me, told me not to move camp the next morning until he got there. I told him that we had several miles of hill to pull and that in order to protect the stock I would have to start moving at four the next morning when it was cool. He was rather arrogant and said, "I'm telling you 'do not move a wagon until I get here' which will be about ten o'clock." I told him that if it was pictures he wanted, he had better be there at four A.M. Sills made the mistake of his life in not being there at daylight, for when the sun came up behind us as we were pulling the long hill, it made a wonderful picture.

We moved on to the Pageant ground about noon the next day. I had ordered hay and grain sent out from LaGrande which was already at hand. We had the parade on schedule; I had a snatch team spotted at one little hill that might give us trouble—it had to help up only one wagon. The Indians attacked the wagon train and we were rescued by a bunch of cavalrymen, all in the traditional blue which had been rented from a Costume House in Salt Lake. The President and his party were treated to a show done up in grand style and Baker and LaGrande started the long painful road of paying off the $16,000 indebtedness which they owed—thanks to some jealous community.

Early in 1925 I was approached by a committee from the American Legion who wanted to support me for Mayor of Baker. As Mr. C. L. Tostevin who then was Sales Manager for the Union Oil Company in Portland had notified me that the company was recalling me to

Portland to work directly out of that office, I explained to the committee that I would not be available. I was transferred back to Portland, again took charge of the refined oil deliveries and was again Salesman-at-large in the city and was to work with and be available at all times to help other salesmen when called upon. I was also to represent the company in public relations work with the Kiwanis Club, Chamber of Commerce and others.

A few years later I was approached by John Farre, who had a small cattle ranch on the Deschutes River, and asked to buy a half interest in his holdings. As cattle work had always been my first love, I bought in with John Farre, buying his other half later on when he wanted to retire. Leaving the Union Oil Company was rather hard to do, for Mr. Tostevin had been very kind to me, but working for myself in a business I loved overcame his pleadings for me to remain. I stayed in the cattle business almost twenty years when I retired, selling the ranch and cattle to Mr. Tom Dant of Portland.

During the years spent on the Deschutes, we entertained numerous boys and girls from Portland and vicinity and around our camp fires were told many western stories which will be told in the final chapter of this book.

Around Western Campfires

"Well, boys and girls, let's build our last campfire and all gather round for our usual evening fun with its music and story telling." Soon a roaring fire was going and we began our usual session. "Mr. Axford, the crowd said, "you lead off." "All right, here goes; my first story will be called A Luger Meets the Colt 45."

For many long years the Colt single-action 45 had been the most universal gun used in the West. The single-action Colt 44 had a very short life among western lawmen for its weakness was soon found; its cartridge shell would sometimes swell in the cylinder when exploded, thereby locking the cylinder so it could not be turned by hammer action. But the West's famous peacemaker, the 45, never failed and, besides its hitting power, would often knock a man down, which, in a gun fight was like a boxer keeping a man off balance so he could not get set to deliver the blow.

Shortly after the Spanish-American War, a new gun showed up in the West, the German Luger; this gun could be fired very rapidly and soon came into use by western officers. In Naco, Arizona, an officer by the name of Otto Moore who had fallen for the new gun spent a lot of time showing it off to others. Moore explained how fast this gun was—one could pour four or five shots in while a man with the old single-action would be getting in one shot. How true this was but what a difference that one shot could make, Moore did not find out until several days later.

A bad situation had developed between the Express Agent in the town and Moore. The agent was an elderly man and had a habit of being a little too abrupt when contacting the public. This was a habit which had been formed over the years by most employees connected with the railroad world—they felt a little superior to the average citizen and treated them accordingly. Anyway Moore and the agent had a clash and fighting words had been passed between the two. The agent told Moore that the next time he came around bothering him he could expect trouble. It was known that the old man had a Colt single-action 45 which he kept in a drawer in his office. Moore laughed when someone reported to him that the old man was carrying the 45 stuck into the waist band of his trousers, and that the old man wouldn't have a chance against the Luger he was carrying.

Things rolled on as usual for several days; Moore stayed away from the express office. However, one day the old man had to go uptown for something and the two met. The agent was the aggressor—he cussed Moore out and told him to go after his gun. They stood facing each other for a moment and then went into action. The old man was wearing a pair of suspenders and had stuck the 45 in his waistband just under the Y-shaped fastener on his left side. In trying to get his gun out, the hammer caught in the Y-part and it was a moment or two before he could jerk the gun loose. Moore by this time had poured six shots into the old man; finally he got his 45 into action.

The one shot he fired, when it hit Moore, knocked him down; by this time the agent was also down but not from the hitting power of the Luger—he had stood erect while taking the six shots. They both died, Moore dying first, but he lived just long enough to know that the old peacemaker could still whip the Luger and give its six shots the best of it.

After this battle, most officers in the Southwest went back to Old Faithful, the single-action Colt 45. However a demand for a fast shooting six of a large caliber caused the Colt people to bring out the Colt automatic 45. The Luger today is considered good for target shooting only and not a fighting gun.

I then continued, "It makes a lot of difference, doesn't it, in a gun fight if one does not get excited but takes his time." Jim Fielder proved that in his fight with Canfield. Canfield, one of the city officers in Silver City, New Mexico, was a rather troublesome type and prided himself on his fast draw with a 45. He was often seen practicing in the outskirts of Silver City, in order to make his draw faster, if possible.

Jim Fielder was one of the better known lawyers, was part Indian. I believe Comanche, and was considered one of Silver City's better citizens. Jim had the odd habit of dry-smoking his cigars, never lit a cigar, but slowly dry chewed until the cigar was gone. Canfield, for some reason understood only by the two of them, cussed Fielder out one day and advised him to keep out of his way unless he wanted trouble. This caused considerable excitement with the town's citizens and many wondered what Fielder would do; some thought that Jim might be forced to leave town rather than face Canfield with his reputation of being exceptionally fast on the draw.

Fielder kept his own counsel, but it was noted that Jim went armed and did not seem to be trying to avoid Canfield, but made no effort to seek Canfield out. Things went on in this way for several days. Canfield made his headquarters in the White House saloon. Silver City had three prominent saloons, "The Red Onion," the "Blue Goose" and the "White House."

One day it was necessary for Jim Fielder to enter the White House saloon, had some papers to be signed, I believe. Jim, with his cigar in his mouth, was immediately challenged by Canfield and told to go after his gun, Canfield drawing at once and starting to shoot. Fielder reached up and shifted the cigar to the left side of his face, and then drew his gun; by this time Canfield had shot twice and was starting on his third. Taking his gun in both hands and carefully taking aim, Jim Fielder made only one shot, hitting Canfield dead-center between the eyes.

Something was mentioned about Bert Alvord and I spoke up. "I knew Bert Alvord, Billy Stiles and Matt Burts," and told this story of the train robbery at Cochise Station.

Bert Alvord had been a deputy for John Slaughter several years before the robbery at Cochise Station and a few years later found Alvord the Town Marshall in Willcox, Arizona, located on the Southern Pacific Railroad in the northeastern part of Cochise County.

A man named Hood, as I remember it, had been seen with Alvord, Billy Stiles and Matt Burks in the mining town of Pearce, where Hood had spent a day or two talking with the three men. A few nights after the meeting in Pearce, Matt Burks and Billy Stiles held up a Southern Pacific passenger train at Cochise Station, a few miles west of the town of Willcox. It was told around the campfires that Stiles and Burks were after a government payroll on its way to pay off the soldiers in the Philippine Islands. It seems that what Stiles and Burks did not know was that the passenger train was running in two sections, the first section carrying no money, the payroll being on the second section. The boys stopped the first section and missed the payroll. This was a robbery that everyone expected, Hood having been seen in consultation, was known to have some connection with the railroad and suspicions had been aroused.

So, a few days after, when Alvord was arrested and taken to the Tombstone jail it was no surprise to the natives. I do not remember whether Alvord had been tried and convicted or in jail awaiting trial when Billy Stiles held up the jailer George Bravin and liberated Alvord. Alvord and Stiles were captured at different points later and I believe both were captured by Deputy Porter McDonald; anyway Alvord was sent to the pen at Yuma, everyone saying that in no time he would be pardoned. Sure enough, Alvord was soon pardoned. Just what connection they had has never come to light but everyone felt there was something rotten in this holdup.

The fire was replenished and we looked around to see who would add the next story. One of the Marshall boys spoke up, "I see where a namesake of mine had quite an experience with his dog," and proceeded to tell his story.

Ben Marshall owned a little ten acre tract of land a couple of miles outside of Estacada, Oregon. Ben was a bachelor, worked at odd jobs for his neighbors and, to supplement his income, kept three or four dozen chickens and a couple of milk cows. Ben had lived in the vicinity for over forty years and until lately the neighborhood had never been bothered by petty thievery which so many times is a problem in more thickly settled communities. However the past several weeks had brought numerous night thieveries in which a number of chicken houses had been raided.

As Ben prized his flock of Rhode Island Reds very highly he was greatly worried about his little setup. Thinking things over Ben decided to buy a shot gun and to keep it close by his bedside, ready for use, should anyone attempt to raid his place. Ben bought a double-barrelled 10-gauge shot gun and a box of cartridges in Estacada and returning to his ranch, muttered to himself as he placed the gun alongside and at the head of his bed, that he would like to see some son of a gun try to rob him.

It was in the summertime and while this beautiful Northwest country is usually not cursed with many days of extremely hot weather, for several days the temperature had been in the nineties. Because of the heat Ben was sleeping semi-raw, that is, leaving off the bottom part of his underwear and using only his undershirt. One night along towards morning Ben was awakened by a disturbance among his chickens. He almost stepped on his dog lying alongside when he jumped out of bed and reached for the shot gun. Slipping quietly out of the house he approached the chicken house cautiously, slipped open the chicken house door and crouched over trying to see what was going on, both barrels cocked and ready. At this moment his dog, coming up behind, poked his cold nose against Ben's rear and, in the excitement caused, Ben pulled off both barrels of the shot gun, killing twenty of his own chickens.

Someone mentioned that he had read an article calling attention to the fact that the railroads were compelled to use spotters on their passenger trains, and that caused Marshall to remark that he had a story to tell along this line.

Several years ago, I made a trip to Alamogordo, New Mexico, which was a division point about 130 miles east of El Paso on the El Paso and Northeastern Railroad. I was standing on the depot platform talking to Ed Maney who was a traveling salesman for one of the big meat packing companies. I had known Maney for several years; also talking with us was the conductor who was to take the train to El Paso. Here at Alamogordo, engine and crews were changed, as it was the division point.

The conductor who had just brought in the train walked up and addressing himself to the conductor who was to take the train asked, nodding his head towards Maney and me, "Are these fellows all right?" On receiving an affirmative answer, he said, "You see that fellow in the salt and pepper suit—well, he is a spotter. His pass number is 'so-and-so'." The conductor wrote down the number. They left us and I said, "Let's get a seat right behind the spotter and watch the fireworks." This we did. In due course the conductor came along and asked the spotter for his ticket—he said he only had a few dollars and wanted to get to El Paso. The conductor said, "Give me what you have," took the money and as he turned away told the spotter, "You and I are both ahead."

After the conductor had passed on, Maney and I went to have a smoke and I asked Maney, "What kind of a damn fool is that conductor—he was warned about this man, yet took his money."

I often wondered about this and several months later running across Maney, I brought up the spotter and asked, "Did you ever hear anything more about this?" "Yes, Marshall," said he, "you could never guess how it came out, but here is what happened. The spotter at the end of the run turned the conductor in for accepting the money. The conductor proved by his report for that day that between Alamogordo and El Paso he picked up pass number 'so-and-so' and the spotter was fired."

Meacham spoke up and said that he had read where the famous John D. Rockefeller was passing through Willcox on the way to the Coast, and was reminded of the following story.

Years ago John D., Senior, and one of his corporation lawyers were walking together along Fifth Avenue in New York City when they were approached by a man showing considerable wear on face and clothing. The man, addressing himself to the lawyer, asked pleadingly for a sum of fifty cents. "Why do you particularly ask for the sum of fifty cents?" asked the lawyer. "Well, to be frank with you, I need the fifty cents to buy some whiskey to help me to sober up."

The lawyer immediately reached into his pocket and handed the man a fifty cent piece. The pair walked on together for about a half block when John D., clutching the lawyer's coat sleeve, stopped him and asked. "Why did you encourage that type of a man by giving him fifty cents?" "Well, I thought his honesty and good judgment entitled him to some consideration." "What do you mean—his honesty and good judgment?" "Well, he certainly was honest—he said he wanted the money to buy whiskey with, and he surely showed good judgment by asking me instead of you."

This story produced a good laugh and Meacham went on, saying, "You all remember Ezra Meeker."

Several years ago Ezra Meeker fitted up an old time covered wagon with a team of trained oxen and retraced his way back over the Old Oregon Trail. The newspapers were full of this famous trip being made by one who had made the trail west to the Oregon Country in earlier days. And old Ezra was entertained and photographed many times in his slow progress across the country retracing the old trail.

Ezra finally reached Washington, D. C., made his way to the White House, stopped his oxen and wagon in front and went in to see the President. The President's Secretary tried to explain to old Ezra that he would have to wait from thirty-five to forty minutes before President Coolidge would be available. "You go right in, young man, and tell your President that I am ninety-two years old, have driven my oxen clear from Oregon to see the President and I don't have thirty-five or forty minutes to waste."

It is said that President Coolidge did not keep him waiting.

Meacham then added the story about the committee which was to pass on the New York Stock Exchange Building. The new building was finished and an acceptance committee of several members had been appointed to look over the building and make the necessary report before the building could be accepted and the final payment made. This committee, consisting of members of the Exchange, had among them one man who had a tendency to stutter when excited but he was also a famous wit. The committee had looked over the ground floor and was proceeding up the grand stairway and stopped to look over some pictures which had been hung on the first landing. The pictures were of famous members and included among them a picture of Jay Gould and one or two others. The committee stood in silence for a moment when the stillness was broken by a stuttering remark, "Wh—wh—wh—Where's Christ;" It is needless to add, in the days of Jay Gould and others of his type, a picture of Christ would have been entirely out of place.

The story about Teapot Dome was told by Shorty. It has been said that the Teapot Dome scandal was purely a political one; that one man's treatment of President Wilson when lying sick in bed so aroused certain members of the committee who had been sent to demand Wilson's resignation that they swore revenge. The story goes that when the committee, practically forcing its way into the President's sickroom, was surprised when one member of the committee walked up to the bed, jerked the bed covers off Wilson and told him to quit playing sick, to get up and take care of his duties or resign.

When learning of the rough way the President had been handled, the Democrats watched carefully for a way to get even. Noting that a large sum of money had been borrowed by the offender from a noted oil promoter, they quickly built up a case and the famous Teapot Dome scandal was on its way. This man was tried and convicted and his usefulness as a public servant destroyed. The trial allowed the oil interests who had made a bad bargain with the United States Government to get off the hook and saved them from a substantial loss. For the government had driven a shrewd bargain. Teapot Dome had not proved the great oil field which was thought to exist and the company would have had to build immense storage tanks in various strategic parts of the world in order to live up to its contract.

The scandal served two purposes; the lease for Teapot Dome was cancelled, thereby saving the oil interests millions of dollars; and revenge for one man's treatment of President Wilson was achieved.

Then Shorty went on with another story. In traveling across country one time, I stopped at a small country store to buy some luncheon supplies. In entering the store I had to walk between two rows of sacked salt, one on each side of the aisle. The counter was heaped up with salt—in fact, there was salt everywhere. "My Lord!" I said to the old fellow behind the counter, "you must sell a hell of a lot of salt." "No," he said, "we don't, but that salt salesman sure did."

"Well, Axford, it's about time that you added a story or two."

So I told them about the time that Professor Douglas, head geologist for the Phelps Dodge Corporation was said to have turned down what afterward became one of the richest copper mines ever found—the United Verde.

Somewhere in the late 1870's, two men located a copper prospect on Mingus Mountain in the Black Hills in the central part of Arizona Territory. The two pardners, John Ruffner and August McKinnon, worked the property for several years and all during this time tried in many ways to interest outside capital in taking over the mine.

The Phelps Dodge interests, keeping tab on the mining developments anywhere in the Southwest and hearing some glowing reports about the Ruffner and McKinnon holdings, sent their top mining expert, Professor Douglas, to examine and make a report on the claims. After spending several days in going over the property, it is told around the campfires that the Professor wound up his report something like this.

They are asking $65,000 for the property; I would not give 65c for it, for in my judgment, it is impossible for an ore body of any size to be in that formation. Shortly after this Ruffner, who had relocated the property, leased the mine to Governor Tritle who in turn was able to interest a Mr. Eugene Jerome of New York who insisted that the town at the mine be named after him. So the town was called Jerome. However, it was not until 1882 when the Atlantic and Pacific Railroad reached Ashfork and when a road had been built from Ashfork to the mine that the real development began.

In 1886, W. A. Clark from Montana bought the property and for years the United Verde outranked any mine in the world in revenue received from its ores. As Professor Douglas at the time of his famous report ranked alongside John Hays Hammond as a mining expert, it goes to prove that when it comes to mining even the best of them can be wrong. Professor Douglas maintained until he died that the United Verde mine was a freak and should not have been in that kind of rock formation.

There is a story connected with the reopening of the Tombstone mines, as follows.

Tombstone was to be reborn. A consolidation had been perfected, the Contention, Lucky Cross, Toughnut and other mines were all now in one big corporation known as the Tombstone Consolidated Mining Company. Immediately all office personnel from the Superintendent down were engaged in planning the operations. Four large marine boilers were to be installed, and station and sinker pumps ordered, for the plans called for the unwatering of the different mines which had to be closed down on account of water. This was big operations. It called for salesmen of all kinds to converge on Tombstone in order to get in on the many orders for material and equipment sure to be needed. It was a common thing to see a salesman dining with some company official trying to interest him in giving an order for his line. The Can Can Restaurant was a busy place. At many of these dinners considerable quantities of wines and liquors were consumed and often both salesman and customer needed assistance in getting to his hotel or home.

We do not know just what company officials made the purchase related in this story, but this is the way we heard it. The big boilers were in, triple expansion station pumps had been installed on the 600 and 800 foot levels, five Prescott sinkers were pumping in the three compartment shaft and the unwatering of the district was in progress. The water line had been lowered enough to enable the Toughnut hoist and shaft to be made ready for operation. A gang of men had been dispatched by Master Mechanic Gordon to clean up the machinery and the Toughnut shaft house. When they unlocked the door to the shaft house they found the entire place filled with fifty or sixty large wooden barrels. They notified Gordon and a couple of office men were dispatched to find out what it was all about. The barrels were found to be full of boiler compound from a company in Syracuse, New York—a full carload of the stuff. Somebody lost his job over this; it was figured out that at the daily rate they would use the compound, it would take fifty-sixty years to use it up. This somebody evidently had had too many bubbles in the champagne served by some salesman selling boiler compound.

I also added the story about Ben Henderson and the complimentary vote. Ben Henderson was one of the world's best neighbors; everyone liked old Ben. He was about average as a citizen, always attended meetings, voted regularly, but every time he got on his feet to talk was completely tongue-tied and unable to speak.

At one County Convention a very prominent citizen had been chosen to run for County Judge and the opposition party was at a loss to find a suitable opponent for this office. They could not think of a man who could match the other party's choice for the County Judge position. At their convention when the nomination came up, at first no one was suggested. No one wanted to run against the other party's nominee. Realizing that whoever was put up would only go down in defeat, they finally agreed to place Old Ben's name before the delegates. As there was no opposition Ben Henderson was duly nominated to run for County Judge in the November election.

When the fall campaign started it was agreed, as Ben was unable to do any talking, a prominent citizen was to represent him and do what he could to help out. At every meeting in the different districts of the county this citizen would get up and present Ben's name to the voters. He always stated that owing to necessary work on the ranch, Old Ben was unable to be present. "You, my citizens, all know Ben Henderson; while we do not expect him to be elected, I do ask each of you who can, at least to give Old Ben a complimentary vote."

When the votes were finally tallied, Ben had been elected by the complimentary votes and the prominent citizen who was unbeatable went down in defeat.

I then told about the real Black Jack—that Black Jack Tom Ketchum was not the original Black Jack, as a great number of people believed. In about 1895 or 1896, four new faces showed up on the San Pedro River Range. One of these, Jesse Williams, went to work for Ed Roberts, owner of the O H brand on the Upper San Pedro. The other three scattered around. One, Tom Anderson, worked for a while for the Boquillas Land and Cattle Company on an adjoining range.

These four men evidently kept in close touch with each other although I remember only one of them, Tom Anderson, called Black Jack, as ever visiting Jesse Williams who was then working for the same outfit where I was employed. Anyway Arizona was suddenly made aware of the fact that a group of desperate men was in the vicinity, for an attempt was made to rob the bank in Nogales. The bank robbery attempt was a failure and nobody was injured, as I remember, in the exchange of shots between Black Jack's gang and the citizens of Nogales.

I had learned from Williams that Tom Anderson and one of the four who claimed to be his brother were the Christian brothers who used to head a wild bunch in the Indian Territory.

This original Black Jack gang did not make much headway as highwaymen, outside of robbing a general store in Separ, New Mexico, and I believe another store in the Morenci country; this was their entire history with this exception—one of the gang was killed in a fight with officers at the Diamond A Company horse pasture in southern New Mexico and Black Jack was killed at a sheep camp somewhere near Morenci. This broke the back of the gang.

I do not believe that the officers who killed Black Jack ever learned just whom they had killed. My information was furnished by Jesse Williams, one of the original gang. Anyway, a few months later, the Ketchum gang consisting of Tom Ketchum, Sam Ketchum, Will Carver and Dave Akins, made an attempted train robbery at Grant, New Mexico and Tom Ketchum waved and called out to someone, "Tell them that Black Jack is still alive."

From then on Tom Ketchum was called Black Jack Ketchum. I knew the entire group—Tom, Sam, Will and Dave—they came to my camp many times when I was working on some copper claims in the Swisshelm Mountains. The original Black Jack was one of the Christian brothers from the Indian Territory. Tom Ketchum was not Black Jack.

I wound up the evening with the stories of Will McGinnis; about the fight at Cimarron Cienega, and when McGinnis was captured.

How Will McGinnis got in with Sam Ketchum and Bill Carver I will never know for when Carver filled me in on the story, I neglected to obtain this information. When I last saw McGinnis he was still working for the W. S. outfit at Alma, New Mexico. From Carver's story, I was able to picture this fight from one of the participants, while what Sam Ketchum told of the fight came mostly from hearsay by others who claimed to know.

It seems that Sam Ketchum and Carver had divided blankets with Tom Ketchum on account of his brutal ways. Dave Akins had also pulled out of the gang for the same reason, and when Tom Ketchum was afterwards arrested for a robbery and hung in Clayton, New Mexico, he was a man discredited by his old gang and strictly on his own.

McGinnis, Carver and Sam Ketchum had made an attempt to rob a train on the Santa Fe Railroad, had cached powder somewhere along the right-of-way, but after stopping the train they were unable to find the powder, resulting in what was known as a water haul in the profession. A posse was immediately formed to go after the boys and overtook them just as the three were making camp at Cimarron Cienega, opened fire at once and before the boys knew what was happening, had hit Sam Ketchum in his left shoulder with a soft-nosed bullet, putting him out of the battle which followed.

From Sam's story, Carver was on top of a little hill and McGinnis was about halfway down the hill. The first volley which had put Sam out of action also hit McGinnis in the right side high up and grazed him across the back of the neck; this left Carver, for the moment, alone to do the fighting. Sam stated that while Carver was fighting hard, he was overshooting and doing no damage. Suddenly McGinnis recovered consciousness, crawled to his 30-40 and started shooting. Sam said McGinnis only missed one shot; he had cut down on an officer who had a part of his rear exposed from behind a tree; just a split second before McGinnis fired at him, he shifted his position and McGinnis missed. Sam said he heard McGinnis say as he missed, "You son of a b—," I'll get you this time," as he pulled a steel-nosed cartridge from his belt, slipped it into his 30-40 and taking aim at the center of the tree, blew splinters clear through the officer crouching behind it. Anyway the posse was defeated by the superior fire of the 30-40 guns; the posse, I have heard, was armed with 30-30 Winchesters.

Carver and McGinnis got Sam on his horse and while Sam begged them to leave him, they refused, saying they would take him to where he could get help. Sam fell off his horse a time or two until the boys finally tied him on, and coming to a ranch house decided to leave him there. The owner, it seems, was not at home. They entered the house and made Sam as comfortable as possible while Sam was still begging them to leave and save themselves. There happened to be in one of the rooms several fifty-pound sacks of flour. Carver wanted to leave, but McGinnis refused. Taking several sacks of the flour, he barricaded the windows and made ready to fight it out, in trying to save Sam, whose condition was steadily getting worse. His constant pleadings that they leave since he would not live anyway finally prevailed and the two, Carver and McGinnis, pulled out and left Sam.

Later when McGinnis was captured at the Lusk Ranch outside of Eddy, New Mexico, at the trial, testimony was given changing the position of the boys on the hill, McGinnis was placed high up on the hill and Carver given the lower position. From the bullet scars on the trees, the jury could easily see that the man down the hill was the one who won the battle. By this switching of positions, McGinnis' life was saved but he was sentenced to a long term in the penitentiary at Santa Fe. He was later pardoned, having won many friends by the courageous fight which he made when captured and with some kind of help from his old pardner, Butch Cassidy.

You will find from the records that Tom Ketchum was alone when he attempted his last train robbery, discredited and abandoned by his brother Sam and Will Carver. Dave Akins had quit on account of Tom many months before in Arizona.

Parts of the story of the capture of McGinnis were told to me by Will Carver who came back to Arizona for a while after McGinnis was captured, the rest gleaned from stories told for years around the campfires about the courageous fight made by McGinnis at the time of his capture.

It seems the original Ketchum gang then consisting of

Tom and Sam Ketchum, Will Carver and Dave Akins, in passing through into New Mexico from their haunts in Texas, had formed a friendship with a rancher whom they called Old Man Lusk. Lusk had a ranch somewhere near the town of Eddy and the boys in passing through often spent the night at this ranch. After leaving Sam Ketchum in the ranch house after the fight at Cimarron Cienega, Carver and McGinnis dropped in to visit with Lusk. After supper the boys rode back into the hills to spend the night and were asked by Lusk to be sure to come back in the morning for breakfast. Old Man Lusk had a young boy about twelve years old living with him at the time.

The Ketchum outfit had often traded horses with Lusk and he had the idea that they were horse thieves, for one or two of the jaded and thin horses which they had exchanged with Lusk had proved, after getting them in good condition, to be top horses, which fact made the old man suspicious. So now when it got dusk, the old man sent the kid into Eddy to advise the officers that the horse thief gang was at the ranch and would be back for breakfast. The Sheriff and two of his deputies came in during the night and hid out in a sort of a cave just across the dry wash in front of the ranch house waiting for the boys to show up in the morning.

The next morning Carver and McGinnis found that their pack horse had strayed and both spent some time trying to locate it. After searching for a while without any results, McGinnis suggested that he ride in for breakfast and afterwards he would ride up on a high hill nearby where Carver could see him and Carver could ride in for breakfast while McGinnis took up the search. McGinnis rode in, fastened his saddle horse to the fence about seventy-five feet in front of the house and went in for breakfast, leaving his Winchester in the scabbard on the saddle. While eating, McGinnis noticed that the kid seemed to be rather nervous and had raised up a couple of times to look through the window. McGinnis raised up and looking through the window saw three men with Winchesters in their hands inside the fence and approaching the house. McGinnis, having only his six-shooter, immediately rose from the table and realizing that Lusk had betrayed him, shot Lusk, saying, "You son of a b—, I'll take you with me." What he did not know at the time, he had shot Lusk through one of his wrists. He then jumped out the door with the six-shooter in his hand and engaged the three officers in battle. He shot one of the officers down, which left two men to face; he had kept track of his shots and knew he had only one shot left. He shoved the six shooter in the waistband of his trousers and raised his hands. When the sheriff coming up reached for McGinnis' gun, he hit him with all his might, knocking him down; he intended to grab his gun, cover the one remaining officer and make his getaway. When he hit the sheriff he jarred open the wound in his right chest which he had received in the fight at Cimarron Cienega and this paralyzed him for a moment, giving the other officer time to bring his Winchester crashing down on the head of McGinnis knocking him unconscious. They then tied McGinnis, leaving him on the ground in the yard. It is said that the sheriff, losing his head, proceeded to beat up McGinnis while lying tied up. McGinnis is said to have told the sheriff, "I may never get out of this, but if ever I do you had better leave New Mexico for I'm coming after you."

Carver, hearing the shooting, rode to where he could look down on the ranch and seeing McGinnis lying stretched out in the yard, thought he was dead. Carver said if he had known McGinnis was alive, he would have ridden in and tried to rescue him. I do not know if Carver would have had the nerve to do this, but if the situation had been reversed and it had been Carver stretched out in the yard, you could have been sure that McGinnis would have come to his rescue. The sheriff, after cooling off, had a different feeling about McGinnis; he admired him for his great fight, for I understand that the officers fired a great many shots at McGinnis, but on account of his weaving and bobbing were unable to hit him. Anyway, the fight put up by McGinnis is one of the great fights of the West and will always be remembered by old timers. What ever happened to Will Carver I do not know as he disappeared from the scene entirely.

The fire was slowly dying; we all sat around in silence for several moments. The Bar J F Ranch was to be taken over by the new owners, but it would leave pleasant memories of the many evenings spent around the campfires telling the stories—tales to be passed on to our children and our grandchildren in the years to follow.

Index